Enclosed is a clear approach to care for ourselves with an unre amount of good for all of us to many restrictions our current societal systems have placed on us as Americans. We can begin working together instead of competing to provide the goods and services that we now enjoy. And we can learn to appreciate everyone who contributes to the good of society, and in turn, we will find ourselves more appreciated.

We can learn to trust each other and to realize that our very lives are held safe in our neighbor's hands, putting us all in grave danger if not for relying on a complete stranger to perform a mere split second tap of the toe or the critical timely movement of two fingers.

And we can learn from the great teachers like Gandhi, Thoreau, Dr. King and Jesus and create a society more in line with their teachings. Welcome to a new order of people that care, participate, come together and grow as a community. This book is dedicated to building a bridge of trust from the American people back to our own government and correcting all of the problems associated with our current economic system.

This book honestly recognizes our impending financial implosion and provides a detailed solution to 100% of it. It also uncovers the secret to truly changing everything as our US Constitution intended.

This is our chance as Americans relating to each other as real people. Realizing the power of many united as one, we can reshape our entire existence. We can remove most of the fear that we live with today. We can embrace the trust that we will find we already have for ourselves.

One person at a time, your country needs you to decide for yourself.

Submitted by: Jeff Vileta
Woodinville, Washington

You make a living by what you get.

You make a life by what you give.

Dedicated to my two daughters Hailey & Tessa,

my entire family

and the health and well-being of humanity.

A Different Path
Authored by: Jeff Vileta

Published by:

Lulu Publishing
Raleigh, NC

A Different Path

Are we ready now for real change?

A societal alternative
and the means to get there.

Table of Contents

			Page
Prologue			1
A letter from the Author			15
Chapter 1:	We all just want to help		21
Chapter 2:	Our Current Path		48
Chapter 3:	Love and Altruism is the Answer		76
Chapter 4:	The Solution		105
Chapter 5:	Our Psyche and Our Soul		161
Chapter 6:	Great Teachings		190
Chapter 7:	Another American History		216
Chapter 8:	Plan Execution		234
Petition			

Prologue

I see opportunity around us everywhere, lest we deny that America is the land of great opportunity? You only need to be aware of the needs of people, have the vision and the heart to pursue filling that need, and the dreams of success are yours.

Well it should be so simple shouldn't it? I mean, if you follow your dream of serving or helping others, it should be, shouldn't it?

If we all do our part and fill a need by helping each other in some small way, then we should all achieve personal and economic success on all levels. What if I said there was a way to do just this? All the while allowing us to build relationships with the people we care about most while personally growing within a healthy community, regardless of your hometown. If our governing, economic, and societal system does not promote the ability of people to fill needs and create goods and services so that we all may use and enjoy them, then plain and simple: the system needs fixing.

If our economic system restricts our children's ability to get the best education, or if our system restricts our parents' access to the best medicine available when we have all the resources we need for everyone, then it is our economic system that is unnecessarily restricting us, and something needs fixing. If for some reason we can't get a road built to unclog our freeways or hire a teacher to keep classroom sizes reasonable, those are the signs that a restricting system is in need of fixing. A real systemic change to both our economic and government systems is due.

If our economic system were ever to force one doctor from a profession he/she loves or prevent their ability to help people because insurance or other factors make it too expensive or too risky to do "business," then something needs to be fixed. Does insurance truly dictate so much of our world, what we can and cannot do?

Recently I saw two lifetime dreams fail in my community. The first one was a candy shop that brought delight to every child and parent that walked in. Talking with the owner, he had shared it was his lifetime dream. You could see their heart in the store in every nook and cranny, and in their smiles. The other was a music shop where the owner/founder truly shared their passion of music. You could hear it in his voice when you shared with him your favorite artist or some songs that you may be looking for, and he would take you right to it.

In our hearts we know that the greater majority of people create a business to provide a product or service in hopes that others might find a joy in it like that of the spirit of giving at Christmas. These dreams of providing service to their community died because our economic system would not support them.

In our world according to the UNICEF foundation, 24,000 children die daily due to poverty. Combine this reality with a homeless kid population, a nation spending itself into bankruptcy, a timeline history of more war than peace, and if we look around us there are many things about our current society that we simply shake our heads at and know that is wrong. If you believe there may be too many things that are simply not right with our society, then my hope is that you are open to an alternative.

We all thirst for change. Most of us have an idea of what kind of things we might change, but going about it, most simply don't know where to start. The change we thirst for is systemic. A change of this magnitude is not easy to accept because of so many unknown factors.. Some may even call it radical.

Beyond a campaign slogan, most of us don't know what that change would really look like, let alone believe that it could possibly ever happen. This book is a chance at a grass roots movement where we can all speak with one voice and use the system designed within our Constitution to unite and try a different road. A path where trust replaces doubt, where love replaces fear, and the contempt that money created is replaced with appreciation. The change that we seek is more aligned with who we are as people.

Do we really believe that the right budget cuts, a tax break, or a new committee meant to study the effects of a business, healthcare, or social security reform is enough? Do we believe that a new Presidential candidate can truly fix what needs to be fixed? Or are we ready for real social and political change here in the United States of America?

This book is a real life, eyes wide open approach to making America the clear leader of the free world once again. We are free Americans, and we know that anything can be accomplished when we unify behind a cause! That's the beauty of a government by the people for the people, at least if we choose to raise our voices.

We have seen financial collapse recently in Iceland, Portugal, Spain, and we the United States are riding a tidal wave of expenses that cannot be sustained. It is not a secret that these financially catastrophic consequences that our Congress and Representatives are all aware of can bring the end of our country. Yet, it has been coined so "inconvenient" that they refuse to talk about it. This isn't anything obscure that we may have not heard about. There is a problem with Social Security and Medicare/Aid systems that we simply cannot sustain and provide for in our current economic systems. It truly makes me wonder if our informed government leadership has lost faith in the economic system in which we use to serve our country and simply hopes that the market will correct itself. We are seeing cut after cut, state after state in the red, pension plans in jeopardy, and fiscal cliffs approaching. With this, it is obvious that the economic system is in grave trouble.

We have seen a country unite on 09/11/01, and I believe we have seen complacent selfishness before that event. And now in the midst of an economic crisis, we see what it is like to live in fear. It does not take a catastrophe or a war for our country to unite. What it takes is shared vision. Let us remember the hope that filled us when we first elected President Obama. Look at the hope we had when we shared a vision that we can all get behind. It takes a movement with a roadmap we can understand and a belief that we can get there. But the hope soon plummeted realizing that without real systemic changes, no leader can provide the change we desire when their real job is to figure out what to cut.

I share with you a story of an old African man who, lying on his death bed, calls his family and neighbors together to share one last valuable lesson. With the group of people gathered around he reaches into his bag and hands them all a short sturdy stick. He asks them all to break the stick. The sticks, though strong, are easily broken. Even the smallest child snaps hers in two. Then he reaches back into his bag and hands them each a new stick and says to them, this is how I want you to live after I am gone. Find someone to band the sticks together in groups of two, three, or more. Now break those bundles in half. No matter how hard they tried, the bundles could not be broken. "We are strong when we stand together," he says. "When we are with another, we cannot be broken." The lesson he shares is that when a soul is alone, it can easily be broken. If we can first begin by believing there is another way – then united together, amazing things can happen.

It is with the understanding that America united, America educated, and America shown the path of righteousness using the systems that are in-place coupled with a spirit of non-violence, that anything can be accomplished. We are human beings hard wired with the desire to work for the betterment of others and with an innate desire to be appreciated. If we can open ourselves to making a systemic modification to align our societal systems up with that, we open ourselves up to an oasis of possibility.

> *A human being becomes human through*
> *other human beings.*
>
> Zulu Proverb

The reasons for this book are many. Simply turn on the news or open a paper. I was at a vendor of mine that do customized embroidery. Patti and both her son and her daughter work with her as well as employing another half a dozen people. They are so nice to work with and can always be counted on when you need something in a hurry. Unfortunately, one of her big clients had lost one of their clients, his

5

financing backed out, and she got stuck with $30,000 worth of open invoices. She had been fighting back and working for months without paying herself. Three weeks before Christmas, I went into her shop and she looked up at me with a tears welling in her eyes. She said, "I am going to have to find something else, this ain't cutting it." I ask why, when a family that is willing to work hard, they have a great product or service to offer the community, – then why should we punish them as victims of the system?

What do we really gain when our work environment is accurately coined a dog eat dog environment, when we get up to face the grind, and just being a part of the rat race. Will someone please show me an industry that is not cut-throat? Because that would be where I would want to work. To be required to put the dollar in front of the service or the quality of the product is illogical, and I am here to stand up boldly and say that, yes, something can be done. Almost the entire first section of any newspaper on any day is filled with reasons we need a change. Heck, the news should be rated for mature audiences given the violent content. One particularly ironic story should be enough to inspire anyone to attempt fixing the economic and societal systems we live in. One such story is that Group Health's (a major hospital and care provider here in the Northwest) nurses and support staff were striking not too long ago because they could not afford their health care insurance premiums.

Open the newspaper for yourself and see if you can find some reasons why we need a real change. Within this proposal, there is power to start a movement. This is as grass roots as it gets: one man from Woodinville, Washington, sharing a vision and a detailed plan of how to make our country better for everyone. This is a true solution to most of the problems we have. A simple idea shared with another person, you the reader. In hopes that I can find another to raise their hand and say, "I agree. It is time for real change," and sign their name. Not just another piece of legislation or a new politician, but a true systemic modification of our government and economic system and a clear view of not only the possibilities, but a road map to get there and a way to get started right now. I have always been a man with vision. I have always wanted to see the big picture and understand how I best can contribute, and no matter what, I have never been one to say, "I don't know." I always have an idea, as I believe most of us do. I believe we all have experienced the clear distinction between approaching anything with love versus fear. It makes sense that when we think about change we should be thinking with love and looking closely at some of the great teachings from history when rethinking a design of societal structure.

My current chosen profession is that of recruiter, helping companies find the talent they need to grow. Additionally, for nearly 10 years I ran a promotion and marketing company creating ideas for clients. To be of value to my clients, I have to provide ideas that are unique and provide creative solutions to unique challenges. I must look at challenges and objectives creatively and begin by understanding the situation and what we are trying to accomplish. Then I must provide creative solutions that make sense for that company, that situation, the right idea, bringing the right resources together to make solutions happen.

This is part of who I am and part of why and how I approach this book. I am applying these same principles of logical creative ideas to the challenges that our country and even the world is seeing. Never have I been one to simply complain about anything without having an idea. In fact, I have always had a creative anecdote on how to make it better or be willing to try to do something. Whether it's giving a kidney or helping with my daughter's school, I know what it means to give from the heart, and this book is from the heart to the people of the world. We all should benefit together.

Like most of us do, I believe we take initiative. We have creative ideas, smart solutions, and we can all be trusted with the controls of a 2000-pound missile. Collectively, if something needs to be done, I believe we can be counted on whether it's building sand bag walls in the face of a flood, searching through rubble to save a life, or helping build a new road. All of us doing our part, all of us trusting each other and taking part in the things that interest us, weaving the fabric of our society — that is what we're talking about here.

I am willing to do my part. I am willing to share ideas and discuss them. In my experience, when we have a direction and share ideas with each other, whatever we are working on together becomes better. That's how I approach this endeavor. Your input and efforts are not only welcomed, they are appreciated, and they are required.

I feel the same way about our community, our country, and even world issues. Yes, there are some grim issues looming on the daily horizon, but there is really a way to solve them, to create peace and harmony, and to provide opportunity, stability, and prosperity for everyone. We can all have a greater sense of appreciation and community and live within a sense of altruism – sharing and receiving gifts of the heart.

Within this book is a clear path of how we can use the government structure that was put in place by our forefathers to join and band together making three simple amendments to the document that holds our American society together. In this, we can truly change everything in a manner that is aligned within innate desires, aligned with our hearts. We have the power. It is right there in Article V of our Constitution.

I do not look at the glass half anything. I look at it as maybe I have had a few sips, but the gallon of milk is right there, and if it needs to be filled up again then I will get some more. I have heard it said that the ocean does not care if you take a thimble or a million gallons. There is abundance all around, and it has been studied that, except for a few molecules that have went with the astronauts to space, there is the same amount of water on this planet now as there was a billion years ago. Everything has been provided to us. We are at a place in society where we can either harness and enjoy this abundance, or we can allow technology and a world economy to make the workplace more competitive, more cut throat, and the employees more of a disposable workforce. Which would you choose?

One may be confused if we read the paper on a daily basis. You will see headlines of economic crisis, war, corruption, murder, bankruptcy, legal proceedings, and many other stories that could raise concern that our world is simply deteriorating. Budget cut after cut, when is the last time we heard about program expansion besides maybe the expansion of foreclosure programs? We continue see cut after cut to the programs that help make us communities, that fuel growth. A whopping 96% of our states are just beginning to watch serious budget shortfalls where cuts across the board are common place. It is so visible that we all see it, and we wonder if this is something that can be cycled out or is there truly an economic growth that can bring our government budgets back in the black?

On the other hand, one only needs to go a little league game, attend soccer practice, or watch a PTA in action to remind us of how much good there is all around us. A block party with our neighbors, planting bulbs in the fall for spring flowers, dinner with our family and friends... these are all part a long undeniable list of good things that occur around us on a daily basis. A lot of the good things happen at the community and family level. Amazing change can happen at this community level when we realize that our hearts are the same. As we look back when President Obama first captured the election, there was a renewed hope like we had not felt in a long time. Maybe it was because we as American people showed that we could use our voices and our votes to break racial barriers, even break a bit of the "establishment" if you will.

But no matter who is elected President, he or she is still working with the same failing economic system and the same government structure that we have a hard time trusting. Until we can make true systemic changes to our economic and government systems, we will continue the cycle of pinning our hopes on a challenging party that promises change. But the truth is that without the people speaking, true societal and systemic change will never really happen.

I have also made some observations regarding the left and right sides of politics. It is evident that there are plenty of loyalists on both sides. However, I believe the general populous want more than empty promises, regardless if it is called conservative or liberal. We all want something more than what any one candidate or party or even voting in an entire new Congress could provide. I cast my vote, but I have much doubt if it really will make a difference considering we continue to work with the same government and economic systems. I find it difficult to find anyone ready to believe that true systemic change can happen. We just hang to hope.

For many of years, I have heard of people voting for the lesser of two evils. None of us feels that there is a candidate who can institute real change. I boldly say, "Until now." The right leadership, a clear vision, and executing a plan can change our country and have a profound effect on the world in which we live— a world where you and I live the prayer of doing the work to create a place here on earth as it is in Heaven.

This doctrine is about providing more. It is about putting the power back into the people's hands and taking it out of the lawyers and big corporation who have ruled American government. Call it a revolution if you like, but there is a way to make a change provided by our Constitution. The power lies within three simple amendments. This book is a detailed plan to make systemic changes to our economic and political system so that a governing body is not only clearly represented by the citizens, but also works to serve the people.

It is time we take advantage of our revolutionized communication systems and many other advancements that were created as improvements for our lives. These improvements should translate into more quality time with the people we care about or provide an opportunity to be more creative. Here is our chance to change the fact that America is the least vacationing country. Here is a chance to build a bridge not only to our government, but back to the people that mean the most. It is time to embrace the creativeness and ingenuity of our people and to let go of the fear that we must live with another "downsizing" or that our job is in constant jeopardy. Let us change our disposable employee society into one of appreciation for each other's contribution. Let's instill pride in community and make it work for us by replacing fear with love. As it has been sung and as the truth has been revealed, only love can conquer hate.

The current state of technological advances, manufacturing process improvements, and new understanding of biological and health sciences have given us a whole new hope that we can provide for ourselves with efficiencies that seemed beyond our imagination 50 years ago, not to mention 250 years ago when the doctrines of our country were originally written. The minor modifications and amendments that have been made to our Constitution are baby steps considering what we have accomplished as a society. Many laws have been created to help restrict and protect ourselves from ourselves. As any corporation that has existed in the past two centuries has found, if they don't reinvent ourselves, they we will not be market leaders for long. Undeniably the same is being held true for our country, and as the world trends are revealing to us, it also applies to our world economic system. We are one of the hardest working countries (though I think most of us would like more time with our families), we were once the "richest," and arguably the most innovative. Yet our standard of living doesn't reflect all the positive aspects that may go along with that. Take for instance the World Tourism vacation day comparison: Italy-42, France-37, Germany-35, Brazil-34, UK-28, Canada-26, Korea-25, Japan-25, US-13. Would anyone in the US like to improve this statistic? Even with our President Barack Obama who brought so much hope, most of feel that there is no hope to improve our vacation ranking. This is especially true when we have become simply grateful to have a job. Within this book is a way to improve the amount of quality time we have for ourselves and our families, and overall, the quality of life. This plan will answer these questions, and it will help guide us to the future that we choose. It will open the door to all possibilities. What gives religion so much influence, and what gives the dollar you hold in your pocket the value it has? Until you *believe* in the confidence of its value, it isn't worth anything (just ask a person from Iraq about the value of their country's dollar). If we thought that our country was bankrupt and could no longer pay the interest on our debt, then that dollar might be viewed as having equal value to the paper it was printed on. A tsunami or other natural or man-made disaster could dramatically change the perceived value and trust we have in our currency based economic system. Another direct hit storm brewing off the Atlantic coast might be just enough to shake our confidence in our government system, giving us the choice to cower into poverty, succumb to a communistic dictator, or worse. Maybe now is the time to climb onboard for a real change, one where we know that we are prepared for anything. If we are willing to provide the assurance of insurance to each other, the confidence that we are willing to and want to help others collectively as a country, then we have something very special. It is the perceived *belief* in the truth that makes it such a challenge for real change. I understand fully the magnitude of what change is being outlined here. But just as Martin Luther King believed, I also believe in the power of all people when given a chance to do good things. You must realize that we are all much more alike than we are different, and that within us is much good, much caring, and much love. We all want to show real compassion and be appreciated. Within that trust is the catalyst for a real change to a community, to a whole country. Through understanding, confidence, and a leap of faith, we can change everything. We can remove the fear of having the means to care for our parents, ourselves, and the future of our children. We can embrace all the resources, the many unique products, and the creativity of services that we offer each other. Within the human spirit is a person that wants to help, and we are more ready now than ever before to help by doing, not by simply writing a check for the next worthy cause or disaster area. Show me a cause that needs help, define what needs to be done, and I'll show you hundreds of men and women on the doorstep ready to lend a hand when they know it will benefit our fellow man. Show me an impending flood, and we see a community coming together to doing what they can to minimize the damage.

One individual at a time united together with an idea and a plan has all the power. We must return to the belief and premise of government for the people by the people. Our Constitution gives us the power to change everything. It was made that way, and it was intended to be used to change the governing systems in which we live to fit the times. The government changed so that it can truly be a servant of the people, not a servant of the self-interest of corporations trying to please their stockholders. The truth is the government is filled with those that want to serve; it should be given free rein to serve, not restricted by shortfalls in the budget.

With a shared vision, clear plan, and solid leadership to make it a reality, the power of possibility is upon us. This book is about providing that vision and that possibility of a different path, and I as the writer remain open to serve in any capacity that will best benefit my fellow man. I personally invite everyone to share their ideas. Your willingness to help means you are welcomed in a place of appreciation.

14

A letter from the author ….

I believe in the power of each and every individual. To coin a phrase from the movie Braveheart, "I believe that if we are to choose, we would choose to raise crops and a family – to live in peace and stay out of the troubles." We all want peace; the notion of peace connects us. But like fixing poverty or having faith in our government, we have trouble trusting that it is possible without divine intervention.

But what if there was a way? What if through the simple notion of the petition process we could open all of the doors to all possibilities? The movement detailed here asks for your signature, a sign of support, a sign that your heart would be willing to contribute to your community and your country, that you would support and accept living in a welcoming community of appreciation.

This book reviews some of the current trends while revealing some of the secrets and the truths that our government officials know about our budget problems and refuse to discuss. We as people sense that our current economic system is not sustainable. The promises we have made as a country and the credit card used to pay for them right now make our current financial system simply unstable and unsustainable. This is something we all know, and we are going to continue to feel the pain of the program cuts, inflation, and many other truths that will come to pass as our economic system heads down this road to failure.

I believe we all know that our macroeconomic system cannot be fixed by growing our way out of it. New energy is not the product to offer huge growth markets and the jobs that we hope for. What we need are methods to sustain. We should really be focusing on sustainability to live in harmony with our planet.

The austerity that we are experiencing at all levels of government is a trickledown effect of national debt that has sailed past $18 trillion and when coupled with the unfunded promises of Medicare and Social Security, the cuts will continue to grow and will to tear away at the programs that make up the very fabric of our communities (with senior centers, libraries, mental health, sports, and arts being among the programs going under).

We all share the same feeling that our country is on a crash course and we are completely uncertain of what the other side of bankruptcy will be like. We are not sure what our country might look like, but it does not sound pretty. The secret to the power of true systemic change that can head off this crash course is written into our Constitution, and it is about to be revealed.

A movement of logic has never been more required than right now, while we are still empowered as a free nation. Hopefully, change will come before it's too late. Hopefully, we don't have to learn what is on the other side of a bankrupt country that props the world up. Think of the chaos of a collapsed dollar. I propose to propel our country into a position as world leader of a free nation. A nation that could truly liberate the world of its 60%+ poverty rate, where we grow equality, and we close the chasm of the few rich people and the many that struggle.

I am a down to earth average Joe if you will, and I am very much a realist. I believe the people that are reading this are as well. I am not claiming that there are not bad people, but a few should not hold back the greater majority of us from embracing the beauty that is community. Do we hold ourselves back from receiving medical attention because there may be a few bad doctors?

What I am proposing is a movement in logic that comes from the heart, not from fear or a search for power. By understanding the power of the united and the systems that are now available to make real change, we know that when we approach anything from love in our heart, we will be successful. Alternatively, when we approach anything from fear, it is destined to eventually fail. These ideas of revolution come from love for my fellow man and a desire to grow and feel connected to community. The changes proposed here are tied to our makeup as humans and the lessons of some of the greatest thinkers in history.

As with any project or event where we get people involved; the event needs to be done logically so that it can be understood by everyone. As a Creative Director, my business ideas have to be original and understandable to make a connection and to be appreciated by my clients and their client. As I have mentioned, I am an average Joe who has laid out a vision of love, creative ideas that are grounded in logic and understanding and I ask for God's grace in my mission to share this societal possibility.

It is that connection of the heart that yields the power. It is this power that God has given us. This power of love, in fact this love has been referred to as equal (God is love) and if in fact God is love, then it is this power that we all have. When used, love has unlimited potential to do good things.

It is with that love that I study the sense of altruism and part of the details laid out in this plan for change that are based on giving from the heart. My belief is not in capitalism, socialism, or any form of communism. It is altruism that holds the key to a society that is more in-line with our innate desires and the true hope we have of "change." It is altruism that makes us as a country able to look at a contribution system as a method of allowing everyone to contribute, and likewise altruism provides for a means of an economic system where we are truly given endless possibilities. It is a sense of logic, realism, and the study of how we are made up as a people that keeps me grounded with the facts.

It is my understanding of people, the close connection we have as humans, that gives everything a sense of realness. I believe, and it is continually proven to us, that we as humans are much more alike than we are different. This is reinforced as we come to know the people around us and the commonalities that we share. It is our understanding of what is innate within us that make this plan logical, doable, and aligned with who and what we are within our desires and needs.

I propose we explore a society based on love and altruism. Let's refuse to live with a governmental or economic system based on fear. I witnessed the 2004 election being won on the promotion of fear. We as Americans are warriors; when stirred, we will fight. I would not want to be the enemy against our country. Capturing that warrior passion, consider what we saw during World War II. Everyone came together from battle to rationing foods. Consider how all of us were ready to take our part in battle after 9/11. For the change we desire, we need to have confidence in each other and that the crowd will gather at the riverside of an impending flood. For the good of all, we are needed in the sandbag chain of American possibilities. I make this plan available in every way, in every town, and organization in hopes within our country we find every state, every county, and every city governments coming together to build a community of love and appreciation. We ask ourselves to endorse a petition of real change, so that we can set in motion the wheels that make it possible for us to vote and make what we desire the law of the land.

I make myself available and I believe the greater majority of people in their hearts simply want to help their fellow man. It is part of who we are made up as a people.

I accept everyone's help and ask the question, "is it possible that we can commit our heart to true change?" I can say with full confidence that it is indeed possible. If you share my sentiment, then please sign the petition. Please make copies and seek support. We seek to create a national unified movement of a million signatures in each state to call on our state legislators to demand of congress an Article V Convention as outlined in our Constitution. This convention will give the people the power to influence and make the three amendments described here in *A Different Path*. If we were to ratify the bills into Constitutional amendments, we could truly change everything.

Jeff Vileta
Woodinville, WA

Chapter 1   We all just want to help

Man was put on this earth for two reasons – to survive and to learn. We have used these key fundamentals to evolve, to create tools, and to not only learn to survive, but to thrive as we combine these fundamentals with our innate desire to serve each other.

We can all join our hands in saying that we want the human race to survive. It is the most basic of instincts. Together, we as individuals and families also want to live in peace, harmony, in community, and in a place that not only allows us to care for one another, but allows us to be cared for. I think it is fair to say that we desire to live in a place where we can contribute, be appreciated, and be a part of something greater than ourselves on many levels.

Survival motivates us to hunt or to work to ensure that we can buy food, to have a home, heat, medical care, and enjoy the many good things life has to offer. Survival motivates us to make sure we have enough resources so that we will be cared for throughout our entire lives. If we are lucky enough to have children, we may desire to pass on a better life and open up doors of opportunities for them. To teach our successors in hope that we can have an impact in the world. Survival is how we are related to every other animal on the planet, and it has brought us a long way, evolving from the advent of fire to our current communications system. Additionally learning is innate within us; we find fulfillment in both learning and sharing our knowledge.

Teaching skills and watching others learn and become better people is something we all take great pride and pleasure in. This learning and sharing of knowledge is another means of connecting us. It connects us to a higher place, to a place greater than ourselves, and to each other past and present. Finding fulfillment, such as teaching, connects us to finding our purpose in life.

Part of our purpose is tied to finding out what we are here to learn. What do you feel that you are here to learn? We grow as people while life becomes revealed to us. The continual succession of daily lessons, that which we choose to keep and that which is discarded from our experiences, are what shape us as humans. The knowledge that we seek helps define us as people, both as a group and as individuals. By using or sharing this knowledge to serve mankind, we become who we are designed to be. We in America also have a fire lit early in our development. Earlier and earlier in life, our parents see the need to instill that of being and doing your best, to ensure that we practice daily for hours on end at our chosen field of competition, so that we can be the best. We as parents are torn between allowing our children to compete simply for the sake of competing and to win – while trying to instill a sense of what it takes to win. But when it comes to serving our fellow man—what works better: competing or working together?

We learn to sacrifice what is often necessary to ensure that we put ourselves in a position to win. It is difficult to teach our children to be gracious losers, when it's the winners who are most revered in our contemporary society and we learn that old adage, "To the victor go the spoils." But part of the problem with the current competitive system is that it does not allow us to be on the same side when it comes to the service of mankind. The lines become blurred between friendly, fun, sporting competition to where we want to crush our opponent, and this leads to having over 30 companies fighting for one piece of business. Every industry has become "cut throat," and the notion of serving for the joy of serving becomes lost because it is so much more difficult to compete over a piece of business than simply work together to solve challenges.

Unfortunately, the theory that only the strongest survive in an economic system has resulted in a road filled with broken dreams of creating businesses that serve. This theory also adds to an ever growing gap between the haves and the have-nots, and now even the biggest of financial institutions are failing. In review of the FDIC bank bailout we begin to see the trend taking place since 2008. When the financial crisis first reared its ugly head, we had 25 banks rescued. In 2009, a total of 140 banks were failing; in 2010, that number climbed to 156 banks rescued. By 2011, we see 90 failed financial institutions, and maybe we see the trend leveling off with only 52 failing in 2012. Yes, eventually the market will "correct itself."

Fear of an economic collapse has become part of our social consciousness. How much can the Federal Reserve lend the world governments money that is made out of thin air? The results are an inflationary climate that will continue to create a larger and larger chasm between the haves and have-nots or what some are now coining as the 1% and the 99%. We continue to try and hold our economy together with what is essentially just a credit card in hopes that growth will provide the cure. Truth is, we all know that growth is not enough; inflation will catch up, and we will continue to see the funding for program after program cut in an economic climate that cannot be sustained.

There will come a time when we cannot afford the entitlements we are so desperately trying to protect; services like Medicare, social security, and many state guaranteed pension plans are now in jeopardy of not having the funding necessary to pay on their obligations. There will not be a cure with our current economic system; there will simply come a time where must walk away from our homes, make tough choices about feeding our family, and hope that our more fortunate family and friends will take us in.

We thought we were borrowing against our children's future, but the fact is that we are seeing the effects already. Coupled with the economic climate data is a changing environment that is creating extreme storms, heat, floods, drought, erosion effects of a rising ocean, and tornadoes in areas they never appeared before. We add the cost of a major community rebuild to an economy that already contains unsustainable obligations, and it is easy to understand why we are a little on edge about our country's future.

When our planet has the ability to provide abundance for us all, and each of us is willing to help make the world a better place, it becomes clear that the economic system in which we live does not make sense.

Let's look for a minute at the theory of competition versus collaboration. There are a number of companies trying to earn the business or the right to serve a need in every industry, whether it represents a product or a service. When purchasing anything, we see many similar companies representing a small portion of competing organizations throughout the world. All of them are willing to sell you that product, and in many instances, it's the same exact product the other companies are selling. I see it like this: if a pile of sand needs to be moved, should we argue first about who can do it better and cheaper or should we grab a shovel and get it done?

In the business sector, we see competition to serve. We see a sales cycle and a bidding process where there are many who did not "win the bid" and are left to continue looking and spending their energies seeking out other opportunities. Direct mail campaigners know that you have to send out 100 pieces of mail in hopes that you find the one that needs the goods or services offered (and 1% is a good return). It is the same with telemarketing; we know that you have to call and get many "nos" before you get the one possible "yes" you were seeking. For us as consumers, that means we need to be bombarded with advertising in the form of mail that almost always gets thrown away, answering the telephone at dinner time to hear the latest credit card offer, or even being aware that our 30-minute TV show is actually 20 minutes after all the commercials. This all translates into a system of inefficiencies. Certainly this type of competition is not aligned with our inner desires to help others. No one likes the pressure of having to sell, and no one likes to be pressured to buy. What we do like is the opportunity to help our fellow man; what we do like is building relationships with people we know we can trust.

Can we at least agree in principle that there has to be a better way? That we could work together to provide the goods and services we appreciate? That we really do not need to be bombarded by wasteful advertising, and that those in the same field could work cohesively with other similar companies? Does this sound like Utopia? No! It sounds like a modification to the societal structures in which we live; it sounds like a modification that is more closely aligned with our human nature.

In our society of competing to survive, our culture has evolved to a point that second place is no longer good enough in America. You will not survive in business being second, because those that win are taught to crush their opponents. The only problem with that theory is that when we choose a field of endeavor, when we look for a career to support our families, we are motivated by a number of factors. We are motivated by helping people. Unless you're a professional gambler, 98% of all individuals want a career that somehow helps other people.

It is in our nature. We are people who give, and while our need for survival is paramount, the need for our work to be appreciated is by far the greatest of all motivations. That is how we are made as people, and when you come to know the individual, you will come to find that we are willing to help if we are needed. If we knew our work was appreciated and our needs were met, we would gladly make societal contributions in an altruistic way. Appreciation for our work is at the core of what we hope for in our workplace. Unfortunately, within the greater majority of our employer/employee relationship, appreciation it is not the most prevalent sentiment when profit becomes the highest priority. Herein lays a plan to modify our current societal systems; a way that captures each of our contributions, whether altruistic or simply needed within the community; a system that provides for a complete picture of what our community needs and desires are; a structure in which we not only work together cohesively for the greater good, but we appreciate each other's contributions.

It all begins with trust. This is same trust that we must show each other as our cars pass, heading towards each other at a combined speed of well over 100 mph with nothing more than two yellow lines painted on the road as a barrier. You must believe in the good of people, because we are all more alike than we are different. Accidents are something none of us want, but the amount of perfection in any one person is something we must accept. When we stop to think, we all ask the same question: Isn't there a better way? When I ask people about and share different scenarios based on the ideas, system design, and societal change that is detailed in this book, everyone agrees, "Oh yea, wouldn't that be nice." But unfortunately, people do not believe it possible to make a change in our society, to our government, or our economic system. I am here to not only state that it is possible but there is a way. All we need from you is to accept it within your heart and endorse your state's petition – that's it. And if you would like to get more involved, there are many ways that your talents and willingness will be appreciated.

We want to know that our contribution to help others has an impact, that someone will enjoy our work, and that we are appreciated. In the purest form of giving, that which is given in an altruistic way is the closest to the heart. When that kind of energy between people is harnessed in society, we find ourselves in a type of utopia on Earth. Something that may sound so impossible to many, but we know we are capable of this.

The fact is, we can use modern technology to put into place a government that is truly by the people for the people. And the same technology can help us foster an altruistic system of providing goods and services. I am here to say that we are without limits, and we are capable of creating a world that is not based on fear and doubt, but based on love, trust, and appreciation for each other in a growing community. As an employee, we may feel like a part of the disposable economy, not much more useful than a cheap, disposable toy in a kid's bagged meal you pick up at the McDonald's drive-thru. We may be "lucky" to have a good paying job, but left constantly living with the threat of losing it in the current business climate, the next budget cuts, an economic down turn, or someone overseas or younger who is willing to do it cheaper. The workplace does not feel like a stable environment. As someone who helps others find employment, I can't tell you how many times I have been told of individuals incentivized to train their overseas replacements. Is this a system of instability and one winner and many losers? Is this really the best we can manage? Is it simply what we are stuck with?

Sometimes as customers, we can honestly admit that we can be too demanding. We become a bit almighty with the notion that we are paying someone to provide a service, and dammit! they should do it to our standards. However, the majority of the time, we are all very courteous to each other, and we care for each other's well-being. For this plan to work, we all need to be open to the concept of being appreciative of goods and services provided to us.

An alternative thinking to the power that I, as the customer, have is that I should truly appreciate the service or products you are providing me with, our best tip being our expression of gratitude for others to see. It is time to explore alternative means of exchanging goods and services. We need something different than a system that strangles us and forces us to cut when there are so many of us willing to add and expand, so much abundance, and so many amazingly creative ideas meant to enhance our lives. The truth is that our current system is much too restrictive.

Money causes strange feelings between people, and it is the main source of a tremendous amount of societal conflict on many levels: marriages, classes of people, children, workplace jealousies, and the list goes on. My personal example is with the bellman. Now I love the idea that someone is willing to help us with our bags and welcome us to our hotel room The entire hospitality industry is absolutely fantastic in that right, but honestly, I'm a little cheap and feel that if I rolled my luggage in, I can probably roll them to an elevator. So, given that I'm a little cheap and feel like I am very capable, I probably would rather save the $5-10 I would normally tip. So, as I give the obligatory tip, I am left to wonder if he truly feels appreciated or resented because of the money factor. Does paying the bellman have similar connotations to that of paying a parking ticket or having to replace a motor on your car? For me, the money factor causes some awkwardness in my ability to truly appreciate the services of a bellman or someone who holds the door for you outside of a hotel.

In stark contrast to the many connotations associated our current exchanges exude, we realize that we find meaning in our own lives through the simple act of helping others. The simple truth is that we want these acts to be appreciated. It is our political and economic systems that restrict our ability to simply give and appreciate the products and services that are available to us.

As our national debt continues to ring up like a supersonic gas pump, we feel the effects of inflation and the instability of the economic system itself. It is budget constraints or our economic system that make things unaffordable, such as community programs or additional roads. It is not our lack of resources or the amount of people willing to help, as is theorized in economic classrooms. We have an abundance of resources and an abundance of people that are willing to help in meaningful ways.

Where we continue to struggle as communities, states, and as a country is in maintaining the necessary budgets for the schools, programs, and infrastructure. To balance the books, what is needed are deep cuts in spending or substantial increases in taxes.

Within economic theory, you must give up something to get something. You simply cannot "have" without making a cut or raising taxes somewhere else. We all share the fear that we cannot simply grow our way out of the unsustainable economic crisis we are in the midst of. Our current economic society and structure has evolved into something different than any of our fore fathers could have imagined only 235 years ago. Needless to say, the people 3,000 years ago who created a monetary system out of necessity, out of confusion, and out of fear, could not see the simple differences of creating a societal system based on love and trust in each other – similar to systems that we see from the native American cultures before European influence. There was no way of seeing that such a system would create poverty, limit our ability to create, and create this huge chasm of haves and have-nots.

Fortunately, our country's founding fathers had the foresight and the wisdom to recognize that when it comes to our system of government, it should be structured in such a way to make concessions for the changing needs of people.. In addition to ensuring that there is a method by which the people can influence the real change.

Unfortunately, as a people we lost sight of the need or the willingness to restructure, and now see that big business and political lobbyists have taken over and provide the direction and influence over the distribution of our government services and resources. The paid lobbyists and corporations influence lawmakers as it pertains to their own self-interest. Not a single bill is passed that is not taxed with special interests. America has become the bastard son of corporate influences.

You may wonder why it is bad that we continue to expand the rights of corporations in their role and influence in our government. Remember that people are created to serve one another – corporations by nature of their design can only serve themselves. The tools that we have helped create as service to our fellow man have in some cases made us so efficient that we may have worked ourselves out of jobs or created a global environment of competition that has moved our jobs overseas where greater profits can be had.

It is possible to embrace these efficiencies and build stronger communities, and the details in this book will outline. The information age is upon us. It has been said that the recent advances of technology have made even more of a dramatic impact than the assembly line. How amazing is it that a radiologist, for instance, can look at images via the internet and give his feedback practically in real time, even serving many hospitals at once? If only Henry Ford could see us now. If these new technologies and scientific breakthroughs are not given unlimited opportunity to grow, then these new abilities and efficiencies will actually grow to hinder mankind by making an even more competitive workplace for the common man and woman. A company or government program that is good for the community one day could become bankrupt or a budget cut the next. We are living within an economic system that has become both unsustainable and unstable. There is an air of instability when we interact with government programs, and even in our own jobs, there is an uncertainty.

Our theory of economics is that it will balance itself out, but no one really knows for sure. Because our entire economic system is built only on theory and like a company's balance sheet, numbers and statistics can be made to support different views or emphasize different facts. With an economic theory that makes people into statistics, projections are only best guesses, so follow an expert's advice when picking a stock. Our world economic system is now a $10 trillion game of chance. Would anyone like to place a bet on whether the value of their dollar will go up or down? Our economy is fueled by $10 trillion dollars moving hands every day, betting on the best return on investment.

Our capitalist society creates many opportunities. I as an entrepreneur see opportunities everywhere; my job as a sales person is that of a solution provider. I listen to my clients and understand their needs, and then I work to provide a creative solution to fill that need. Not everyone has a clear path of what they would like to do. Most of us simply know that we would like to make a positive impact or have a valued contribution to others while making a nice living for their family. Like the lottery, capitalist society is a place to create fortunes. In theory, we have the opportunity to create great corporations that serve the world, offer great rewards, and create them from basically just an idea. The formula is actually rather simple: you find a need or a desire that people want and fill it. If you create enough demand and manage your business well, you will succeed. That is the American dream, and it happens, sadly though 95% of businesses fail within the first 5 years. It is sad to think that the business created out of someone's desire to serve.

Most of us struggle to make a comfortable living, save for our kid's education, and fully prepare for retirement. The fact of the matter is most of us are fearful not just for our own futures but that of the entire country. We all want to be a part of something successful. And we all long to be a part of something greater than ourselves. We all long to have a positive impact and be a part of an ever-growing and close-knit community.

There are many examples of teams at work creating something greater than their individual contributions. For example, if you were on a railroad construction crew, you wouldn't be most proud of the 100 spikes that you may have been personally responsible for. You would be most proud of working as part of a team constructing a railway across the state of Wyoming. You might find yourself proud of the fact that your railway now readily provides supplies to remote areas of the country that had to wait months before. You can feel a sense of pride having opened up opportunities for people and being a part of this noble cause that is bigger than yourself. Participating in sports is a great example of playing a role in something greater than just ourselves. No individual can win at a team sport; he can only play their role as best they can and support those around you. Ask a retired athlete what they miss most, and those that are part of a team will tell you, "the guys," being a part of the team, the comradery, the closeness, the fun of the locker room, not the wins or losses. And it's the coaches that touch on the life lessons that are revered and have the most admiration of their player's. They would reap the most personal rewards.

To further illustrate our point of belonging and being a part of something greater than ourselves, we look to the hospital. If you are a nurse, you may find fulfillment in the lives that you touch and the comfort that you bring. But you may also find a sense of pride in the overall impact that your hospital has on the community and the overall success of the organization. Facts such as "your" hospital saved 200 lives; treats 50,000 patients; delivered 1,500 babies, and accepts 5,000 cases of uncompensated care a year. A sense of belonging and having pride in being a part of something greater than ourselves is a simple fact that gives us a place in our community.

Unfortunately, our society and current economic structure of providing goods and services do not necessarily foster companies that offer a secure place with a true sense of appreciation and belonging. The contract expires, and we picket to get what we want. And it's not just in the factories, but schools and hospitals are all in a place of instability.

No, unfortunately our contributions alone or a successful company being taxed does not guarantee that we can build a much needed roadway system. No, in order to survive within this economic system we need to make cuts to the budget or increase taxes somewhere. How often do you hear of a school, city, state or federal budget being cut or programs being eliminated because it was a line on a spreadsheet? Frankly we all share the same fear of our government system's ability to stay solvent; our federal government has major budget issues. All but four states have similar deficit issues. Conversely, how often do you hear of education, police, or roadways being given budgetary increases? In our Puget Sound community, we actually had one of the largest healthcare providers (Group Health.) Their employees had to strike because of the "budget cuts." The rising cost of healthcare service made insurance premiums too expensive for their staff. Now their salaries when factored into the rising cost of individual premiums were not keeping pace with inflation. So our own healthcare workers went on strike to fight for their right to healthcare. All of us can understand that the rising cost of healthcare is a real issue in our society (unless we are one of the fortunate with employers that have a plan that takes care of it). When applied to the healthcare sector of our society, our economic system magnifies the ludicrous structure we have created. It is the healthcare industry that continues to grow more rapidly than an accepted norm of inflation. It is the economic system of trying to take care of an aging population that threatens the solvency of our country, and frankly, the world.

Taking a further look at the healthcare sector, we find that to compensate for the rising cost of a basic service such as healthcare, we feel the growing strain on our entire society. And because it is a growing need and a cost that is rising above the rate of inflation, it's a service that everyone either uses or at some time will use. It is a cost that affects everybody. According to the National Coalition on Health Care, 16% of the gross domestic product (GDP) was spent on healthcare, and in just 12 short years, the Congressional Budget Office predicts healthcare to be 25% of the GDP. Couple that with 25% of every tax dollar being spent on the national debt interest, and you start to see clearly why we are experiencing a widespread budget crisis.

To illustrate the cycle of economics, we reduce costs by starting with the people. The nursing staffs are reduced, and subsequently, hospital waiting rooms get packed, and the wait is longer. When lines get longer, people get more irritable. Now an overworked staff is dealing with a public that is no longer deeply appreciative of their service. A longer line makes for a frustrated public, and as a result, the demand for contribution and the number of individuals who want to make the sacrifice to be a part of the healthcare community reduces. It becomes an overtaxed, thankless job. It continues to spiral out of control until the theory of supply and demand takes hold, and the "invisible hand" works to try and correct it with rising costs to compensate. Perhaps a piece of legislation will be passed that will fix it all? Did "Obamacare" fix it? Was Hillary Clinton able to do anything? A systemic economic system causes this problem, not the people willing to provide healthcare services, the equipment that is available to them, or even the legislation that regulates a particular industry.

I don't think we need to look at the profession of teaching our children to make the point that the current economic structure has holes. While there are many exceptions in both directions, I do not believe that our system allows us as a society to contribute to our fullest potential or give of the gifts that are in our heart. Nor does it allow most of us as citizens to enjoy life to its fullest potential.

Undoubtedly our current society has fostered unethical and overabundance of competition to survive for individuals and companies. This competition has spawned a cut-throat business environment that simply must serve the dollar itself. Fighting for our survival to contribute in today's climate changes so rapidly that it is hard to predict where we will be in five years. "Job stability" almost sounds like an oxymoron these days. Some of us may remember working for an organization where there was a pride and a comfort in knowing you had a future, and I think most of us would take that knowing that at the end of 25 or 30 years of dedicated service, a retirement pension and a gold watch was our reward. That theory on business economics has all but been removed from our culture, and now even our state run pension plans are in jeopardy of insolvency. What we once counted on, valued, and fostered as company loyalty may all but be extinct. It is now replaced with the notion that the company is not loyal to me, why should I be to it? Or worse yet, the notion that it is not personal that I treat you unfairly or without respect, it's "just business." (Is this how we want to be connected to our community?). The current climate is such that you may change jobs 5-10 times in a decade. Loyalty and relationships in the workplace have been replaced with disposable labor, and employee firing is just part of the norm. Our workplace has taken the lead from professional sports and has simply become a part of our current landscape. I remember as a five-year-old kid hearing that our neighbor had been fired and the awful feelings that I had when visualizing him being tied to a stake and literally set on fire. Never will I accept this as anything less than tragic. But as we watch the example set forth in professional sports, disposability, jumping contracts for the higher dollar, and firing is just common place.

The current economic climate has fostered the need for massive marketing efforts. Where we as consumers are bombarded with phone calls at dinner time, stacks of mail that are thrown away before they are opened, and a continuous stream of unsolicited e-mail. Ironically, I find that most of them are trying to sell us money, whether it be credit cards or a new mortgage. Because we as sales persons and business owners know that to be successful you have to take enough rejection to find that one person who is in need of our product and service. It is simply a known part of the formula that you must send out 100 pieces of direct mail or make 25-50 phone calls to get to that . 1% response. For us as a consumer, that simply seems like a bombardment of offers that gets separated and thrown into the recycling every day. The truth is that part of our system is a great big waste for everyone involved. Additionally, we know as sales people that you have to wait hours on the store floor and talk with numerous people who are really "just looking" to talk with that one person that is actually ready to make a purchase. Sales people are not only rewarded monetarily, but also somewhere there is a real satisfaction of honor given simply from the act of providing a service to someone who wants or needs what we are trying to provide. As a salesperson, it is the satisfaction of helping someone and their appreciation that outweighs the money – and that I can guarantee if the necessity of monetary rewards is removed. Unfortunately, we track the numbers instead of the people that we have helped. Underneath the need for a commission, I will show you a sales professional that really enjoys the helping people aspect of their job. None of us want to be looked at like a "sleazy" used car salespersons. But I know that anyone who has had to make a sales call knows the feeling of rejection and understands the feeling to be looked upon as "sleazy" or distrusted. But that is what we need to do to survive and to provide a living for ourselves and help our families grow.

How beautiful is the thought that each family may be empowered to have the option of a homemaker? It is interesting that the number of homemakers has decreased, and so has the number of homes with a traditional family. Gone are the homes where a parent is home welcoming the children from school, where the household is managed, where dinner can be prepared, and everyone can sit down at the table. Gone are the days where, through the work of the homemaker, there is the product of a strong family unit. How beautiful a thought is it that the "bread winner" (man or woman) can do enough to provide for the family when partnered with a homemaker? Do you believe that if the family is held first as the cornerstone of our society, then that should provide for a strong community and country? Unfortunately, the truth is that we now serve the dollar first, and 99% of us cannot have the homemaker-led family. We spend far more time serving the dollar, and our economic system has grown to the point where the dollar comes before the family unit. It comes before simply providing what is best for us as a community, our family, and even just helping a neighbor.

Our current state of economics does not graciously allow you to contribute in your chosen field of endeavor. Imagine you are widget maker and have developed a useful widget that you are proud. The people you show your widgets to share your useful sentiments. As a creator, you may be grateful that what you have created is appreciated, but unfortunately, as a buying consumer we have come to our first question: "How much?" And then we wonder if we can find someone who can do it for cheaper. Let's couple this with the concept of competition. What if someone has a better business plan and finds a way to create a similar product or provide a similar service and has the money to market and hire a sales force? Now you have created this widget but are competing with big business; you may be proud of your creation and people may have been appreciative. But now you are reduced to being a mere peddler, and likely considering the new business statistics, you are the loser because your business has been crushed by a bigger player. In the end, you are sent out of business and looking for a new means to support your family.

It is amazing to me that the system does not allow someone who wants to contribute to society to do it regardless of age. Our system makes it so difficult and almost humiliating for a senior citizen who may have some truly valuable experience and possibly some real expertise, to find constructive work on their terms. It is sad that those that deserve our respect are actually feeling discrimination because they are older and may want or need a job. Should we just say, "Sorry, that's not the way it works. There may be a job for you at a fast food restaurant?" I am here to say there is a better way to foster creativity and ingenuity and to

43

capture the spirit of people who want to help and make a valued contribution to society in all forms, young, old, creative, and non-creative.

So we are left with many questions before us; would we choose to work in a society where we live in fear of losing our jobs? Or would we prefer to be appreciated for our contribution? If we could choose, would we rather compete or cooperate with others to provide the goods and services that we require as humans, as a society, and as part of a community?

When we seek the answer of competition versus cooperation, we will find both negative and positive reasons why it helps our economics or detracts from a local community. That is the beautiful thing about the *theory* of an economic system in which we live. Within a theory, you can shine the light in any direction you want to help support your position. However, living within an economic system based on theories, no one can really predict the future or the outcome. Remaining a clear thinker that is open to the endless possibilities opens the door of change. We *must* start by opening ourselves up to a real societal change.

When it comes down to it, we don't want to have to compete for our jobs. We simply want to contribute and be appreciated. We don't want to have to struggle to feed our families when we have plenty of food to feed the entire world. It is our economic system that constrains all of it.

We don't want to have to worry and stress that our job will be shipped overseas, because there is someone that will do it for a fraction of the cost. There is no denying the simple things that are common between us: sitting down to a nice meal with friends and family; celebrating the birth of a new child; or mourning the loss of someone we truly love. We all feel happy to watch one of our sons or daughters make a play as part of a team on the soccer field. We all feel sorrow for the individual families and communities when we drive through rural America just to find factories shut down and tumble weeds blowing through the streets of our small towns that may have once been thriving communities. Our communities feel pride when a factory in their town is producing whatever it is we may use as a nation (tennis rackets, creamed corn, chairs, pianos... it doesn't always matter as long as we know that we are helping). If Amana, Iowa, is famous for making refrigerators and microwaves, then that community is going to take great pride in producing the best they can. The component makers that support the Amana Company are going to feel pride in supporting their efforts. Pride in workmanship and being a part of an organization that is appreciated is enough if we know that our needs will be met and we can enjoy the fruits of life, part of which is pride in workmanship.

If you work with your child's school, volunteer in a class, join the PTA to making a difference in child's experience; if you helped build a nature trail, volunteered at a hospital, then you have practiced an act of altruism. I would contend altruism is the best kind of work because it is given from you heart. Capturing this spirit of altruism and working that into an economic system of exchange is what we are talking about here.

If appreciation for each other's work is enough, then we should be able to capture that spirit as a currency and as a society. This is what could bring us closer as a community, and this is what could remove the many roadblocks that restrict our abilities to contribute, provide, and live in abundance. We as people take great pride in being a part of something greater than ourselves. Working as part of a company or community that produces a useful product helps promote good will and fulfillment in our lives so much more than working for just a paycheck. We all desire a good job for fulfillment and security.

I am here to detail not only an economic system, but a clear plan to get from where we are at with a failing economic to a place a system that ensures that we as a people have all that is necessary to survive and are able to enjoy the many pleasures in life.

When we talk to real people, we find a lack of faith in both our economic system and our government across the board. When President Obama was elected, he provided a hope, a hope that was quickly eroded. Our confidence waned as we saw that he was restricted and manipulated by the current economic and government structures. I don't believe any of us think that any one person can do anything or that any one piece of legislation can make a truly impactful change to our daily lives.

This book provides a clear road map, a method of using a petition, and the methods of providing change that were thought out and detailed in our Constitution. I am here to say there is a way to create the change we desire. With your signature as sign of support, we can give ourselves as a nation the opportunity to vote on three Constitutional Amendments that could truly change everything.

It is possible - are you open to real change?

Chapter 2 Our Current Path

We just need to open today's newspaper to see the latest trends and get a sense of how the systems in which we live are impacting our world both economically and from a political perspective. The headlines may read that our macro world is headed for doom and gloom, but hopefully within our micro world we find many good things including the love of our family and friends; community involvement; maybe appreciation for a job; having food and a home; our passions and taking time to notice the beautiful things all around us, such as a flower or the sunset. It seems the daily news covers so much violence and corruption that if it were a movie it would be rated for mature audiences only. Add that to our economic crisis, the discussion of a meltdown, the environment at a point of a critical change, looming war and terror threats... watching the world news can be downright scary!

As mentioned, there is no denying we all share the feeling that there has to be a better way. However, most of us think there is no way to get there without some sort of divine intervention. While the intervention of something divine may make something new, we should remember the words of Dr. King, who shared, "While it is important to ask for God's grace, it is not a substitute for the direct efforts and sacrifice of men." Let us not forget that we as a people created these systems and that we as people can make great changes and create a world in which community comes together versus the current truth where we barely know our neighbor. Let us as a people boldly state that we are not subjects to the prevailing wind, and that we in fact control the winds of destiny.

So, within this chapter we want to look at the major areas that affect our country and subsequently our world today. We want to review where we are and trends that may point us in a direction of where we are headed. It is my hope that with this review that we can all come to an agreement that we are at a point where it is time to take a look at real systemic change and agree that there must be a better way in providing structure to our society. Then we will move on to outlining the path. So let's take a look at our environment, economy, government, corporate America, our quality of life, and even take a glimpse of other societal collapses for good measure.

Environment

We are continually provided information about our planet, and frankly, it is so scary that it has become surreal with the thought that we could be forcing our planet into an ice-age within the next century, or that the rising ocean could force us to redraw the global map. The idea that our planet is warming and the growing list of extinct and endangered species seem to be all but a nuisance as we wait to see what the weather will be like tomorrow. Who has time to worry about our environment when we need to get to work? We need to make sure our families have a roof over our heads and food on the table, so we are forced to put our own daily survival ahead of global, long-term survival. Let's pause here to review a few facts that stress the urgency of our current environmental destiny.

The U.S. Government has funded a $20 billion study group called the U.S. Climate Change Science Program (CCSP). The CCSP works in conjunction with major federal agencies including the Departments of Defense, Agriculture, Interior, Commerce, and NASA, just to name a few of the 13 agencies working together to release a report titled, "Abrupt Climate Change." Contained within this report are some of the following facts:

- Glacier melting has increased two-fold, and this problem only compounds itself by reducing the reflective nature of snow, which makes for an even more rapid melt-off.
- The melting of Antarctic and Greenland will likely lead to a sea-level rise that far exceeds those figures that were previously advised in their previous reports.
- The Arctic ice has undergone a 30% retreat since satellite records began in 1979, and the current models suggests an even more abrupt change in years to come.
- Glaciers on mountains have massively shrunk worldwide.
- Major storms have increased 50% in duration and intensity since 1970. A month before Hurricane Katrina hit, a major MIT study supported consensus that global warming is having a powerful effect on hurricanes, which would explain why we

hear of category 4 and 5 as commonplace now and have run through the entire alphabet naming the storms.

- Our measure of CO_2 levels have risen from 280 ppm during pre-industrial concentration to 386 ppm in 2008 (a near 38% increase). Further data revealed through ice-cores dating back 600,000 years show a direct correlation between CO_2 and temperature. There has <u>never</u> been a concentration at this level.

- Permafrost areas store over 10 times the annual amount emitted from man-made sources, and these regions are showing many signs of thawing. If you look at the 21 hottest years measured, 20 have occurred in the past 25 years.

- The Living Planet Index reveals the populations of land, freshwater, and marine species fell approximately 40% between 1970 and 2000.

In addition to this information, the World Wildlife Fund has revealed data related to our Global Footprint. The World Wildlife Fund released a report stating that we are currently consuming 20% more than our planet can sustain. Factors include:

- Our reliance on fossil fuels
- The spread of cities and destruction of natural habitats
- Over exploitation of the oceans

The understanding of the footprint formula is simple. The world's 6.5 billion people leave a collective footprint of 33.36 billion acres, which equals 5.44 acres per person. To allow the Earth to regenerate our resources with the current population, the average should be 4.45 acres per person. Incidentally, the average U.S. resident leaves a 23.47 acre footprint, largely from fossil fuels.

The question derived from this report is not how much oil is left. The question is how much fossil fuel consumption the Earth can sustain. The Earth does not have an infinite capacity, and to put an exclamation point on this fact, within our lifetime the human population is projected to grow 50% to over 9 billion people worldwide. It brings up the question of population and environmental sustainment in the survival as a civilization. Though we in the United States are by far the leading contributor to carbon emissions, they are quickly catching up in areas of China and India where population explosion has hit and industrial revolution has occurred. We as a world populace are having an undeniable impact on our planet accurately measured by our carbon footprint. This is having significant impact now, and the projections in this area point to a growing and unsustainable problem. "We are spending nature's capital faster than it can regenerate," says Dr. Claude Marting, Director General of the World Wildlife Foundation International. "We are running up an ecological debt which we won't be able to pay off unless governments restore the balance between our consumption of natural resources and the Earth's ability to renew them and very soon." We've come to accept the dominant attitude that if nature can yield something of value to the lucrative engines of commerce, then we should by all means grab it and rip it out, giving

52

the scars left on the planet secondary consideration. Unfortunately, we put economic means over environmental consideration if it means personal gain. Because we need economic gains for our immediate survival, we leave the worrying of environmental impact as "someone" else's job.

Currently the United States is over a 30% contributor to the world's greenhouse gases that directly affect our planet's temperature. We are only one of two countries that have not signed the Kyoto planetary agreement in which each country agree to reduce emissions for the good of the whole planet. The climate crisis is indeed extremely dangerous. Two thousand scientists in hundreds of countries have formed a strong consensus that we must work together to solve this problem. The exponential population growth has put a strain on our planet that is easily defined as unsustainable. The fact is that we have reached a tipping point that threatens our civilization. We are now faced with the fact that tomorrow is today and that we urgently need to do something now, not simply believe our children will provide the solution.

Our Economic System

David Walker, the previous Comptroller General of the United States or our nation's top accountant who has overseen our country's assets and liabilities puts it this way, "We are suffering from a fiscal cancer and living in such a way that is unsustainable. If this is not treated [it] could have catastrophic consequences." Not argued, not disputed, but confirmed by Ben Bernhake, our current chairman. Not argued, not disputed, but confirmed by the senators in charge of overseeing our country's budgets, who recognize that addressing the real requirements of paying down a rocketing country credit card would have catastrophic consequences. So we put this off until…

Our national debt continues to skyrocket, and recently it has blasted by the $16 trillion mark. However, it's this trend and looking to the future of our un-funded promises within Social Security and Medicare that should really scare us economically. We are not talking about 50 years from now; the baby boom shift is now, and no longer do we have a $400 billion dollar surplus that we can borrow from Social Security like we have been doing. When you combine these liabilities and the new prescription drug benefits, our national debt looks more like $211 trillion as reported by ABC news (over $600,000 per person). Our thinking has been wrong in believing that we are passing along a problem to our children and grandchildren and that somehow inflation will make this a manageable number. Our dollar is sinking; property values have plummeted; our retirement savings have shrunk 20%; and the stock markets are volatile to say the least. Not only are we feeling this problem now, the entire world is caught up in this recession with many countries already starting bankruptcy.

It won't be two generations from now like we may have hoped. The tidal wave of economic problems we face as a society is upon us now. Somehow economic growth and the value of the dollar made this an easier problem to rationalize, but the fear is that it has now come time to pay, and this monetary figure may be too great for any economic growth to cover. Currently, it is Social Security funding that has given us a surplus in which to borrow against the past 20 years that has filled the gap of an over $400 billion/year deficit spending budget (as we all know by now means that we spend more than we make as a country.) We don't need to make a business analogy to wonder how long a family, company, or a country can last year after year spending more than it takes in.

Over the last 40 years, if you add the Social Security surplus that we spent that we were supposed to be saving for when that program needs it (now,) you will see year after year of deficit spending. Below is a chart of plotting our balance sheet income versus expenditures, and only one year in the last 40 did we have more coming in than we spent.

Figure 3.1

Now the baby boomers that have been creating that Social Security surplus are not only going to be taking back from that program, but their rising need of government funded medical care is scary. Senator Judd Gregg, a ranking member of the Budget Committee, says this issue alone represents a fiscal meltdown of this nation. Shouldn't this impending issue alone be enough to open ourselves to change? The fact is that when we tack on the Medicare and Prescription Drug obligations we have, these issues are 10 times greater than that of Social Security alone.

Not war, not increased weather devastation, but the turning tide of Social Security and the Medicare/Medicaid obligations is the signifier that this economic disaster is upon us. Do you think this might be a good time to consider a real systemic change? Do you think we might want to open ourselves up to the possibility that there may be a different, better way?

Our current national debt has surpassed $16 trillion and increases nearly $4 billion per day (that's roughly $400/month for every man woman and child in America). In the past, America has used the savings of citizens or sold savings bonds to fund recovery. Increasingly we have used the lending of foreign interests to finance this number. Currently about half of our national debt is held by foreign interests. To give a sense of how large the national debt number is, the entire U.S. economy (2011) is worth $15 trillion. Now we may think that we can grow our way out of it or even relate this to the mortgages we have on our house, but with Social Security and the Medicare issues at hand, revenue is decreasing and costs are skyrocketing. There is a growing list of countries that are going bankrupt, so what happens if the United States is not solvent enough to catch the next one?

Our options are a dictatorship, capitalism, anarchy, communism, or socialism. But this book outlines something different. Do we have enough information to open ourselves up to the possibility of a different economic system? One where we could actually correct the problems associated with this economic system, including our debt? Is it possible to build a system where we simply shoulder that which is required to survive and thrive for everybody and close the chasm of the 1% of those that enjoy abundance and the 99% of us that struggle to pay bills?

According to nationaldebt.org, which keeps up current tabs on nearly every statistic, as of 2013, each taxpayer's portion of the debt is over $145,000. On the total debt owed, each family's portion is approaching $750,000 at the time of writing this book. Do you believe that we can simply fix this by someone carving out a new budget within the existing economic system? Or maybe the time has come for something different?

Here is trickledown economics, shrinking revenue, growing costs and an increasing interest payment, and federal subsidy cuts to state run programs. Do we see any program cuts? According to the Center on Budget and Policy Priorities (www.cbpp.org), 6% of our entire budget for 2010/2011 went to finance the interest on the debt. This was when the debt was near $10 trillion; just half way through 2012 and our national debt has sailed past $15 trillion. There was a time when the great fear was held in check by our debt being a percentage compared to our GDP. Well, our debt has surpassed our GDP.

According to fiscal economics, the theory of bankruptcy becomes real when we can no longer afford the interest on our debt. We as a country are bankrupt, and along the way it will continue to fight off fiscal cliffs and raising debt ceilings. We will continue to be forced to cut spending and programs, many of which we have come to appreciate because of our current trending economic situations. We feel it in a growing inflation, and we will continue to watch as the economic engine that runs our planet's goods and services continues to breakdown.

The preceding was a summary of our federal government's current financial situation; the trickle-down effect has also affected 46 of our 50 state governments that are in the red. We see the tip of the iceberg where pension funds are being "borrowed" from to keep other programs up and running. From the state to the counties, cities, police departments, and school districts, all of us are feeling the "trickledown effect."

Want to see a community cry out? Let a school district announce a school closure because of budget problems; watch a soup kitchen close that feeds the hungry. Drive by a park that had to be closed, a senior center that could no longer be funded, or a fire station with no firemen. And these are just a few examples of the many cuts we are experiencing that make up a community falling victim to budget constraints. Budget constraints directly caused by our economic system. There are so many programs and services created out of need, out of serving, and building community that we have come to appreciate and even rely on, and many of these can no longer be sustained. We are forced to learn to survive, to do more with less. Corporations are forced to go overseas where labor is cheaper, otherwise they simply can't compete. So the spiral continues. Do you think we will see a growth or abundance with this current system?

So many people are willing to give of themselves for the betterment of someone else and for the betterment of the community; it is how we gain dignity. But it is our economic system that restrains us and puts needed social programs at the mercy of someone at a desk who has a pen forced to line out people and programs to make the numbers fit into shrinking budgets. These cuts occur not because there aren't enough people or resources to provide these needed services, but because our economic climate forces budget constraints that make it impossible to continue to offer the level of services we have not only come to appreciate receiving but people appreciate giving.

This book not only provides a solution to the economic issues, but our government's issues as well. Let's take a look at the current state of our government system.

Our United States Government

We need only talk with our neighbors or families about the current state of politics to find that we are in consensus; we simply do not trust our own "by the people" government. While our political viewpoints may be different, we can all agree that our system is corrupted by the influence of money. Our status quo for selecting a President has been to simply select the lesser of two evils, and we all see the cycle of blaming the incumbent party and voting on hope and change.

None of us believe or trust that real change can come about with one candidate or even a piece of the best legislation, and we are losing hope. Do you remember the sense of hope we had when President Obama was elected? He did offer a new sense of possibility, and I believed we had found a new level of acceptance of each other and that a nail had been driven in the coffin of segregation. For a moment we had a renewed sense of unity and hope that real change for the better was upon us.

It is no secret that our government has become not of the people by the people, but of big money by big money and the influence of corporate interest. Ironically, the problem lies in the fact that we all want to do a good job when given one, and there are some very good professional lobbyists, some even writing legislation such as the No Child bill, and others influencing legislators in the name of corporate interest. Our United States government is now based on a system of rule with an underlying and deeply worrisome imbalance of power in society between money and people. Those that influence do so out of monetary greed without regards to moral obligation and what they may believe to be right or wrong for the general populace.

It is a tough balance to do work because your job requires it and try to make yourself believe that what you are doing is right and that you are serving the good of mankind. When we think of Maslow hierarchy, we understand that our jobs are tied to our survival. It might not be all government officials, but the distrust we have in our own government system is evident as reported in the Atlantic, an online news source. Atlantic reported that Americans distrust in our government has reached an all-time low of nearly 80%. That means that 80% of Americans do not trust their own government. Why would anything need to change?

Figure 3.2

In the past, we have heard rhetoric about axis of evils, dictating regimes, and we have gone to war because the threat that there may be a possession of a weapon of mass destruction (WMD). We attacked Iraq because they violated United Nation resolutions. This talk of other countries evil doings is so hypocritical it is almost nauseating. We attacked Korea, Vietnam, and Japan ***before they attacked us. The U.S. government is not only the biggest producer of WMDs, we are also the largest merchandiser of WMDs. Furthermore, we are the only country to ever use a nuclear weapon against another country. We have violated hundreds of U.N. resolutions, and we have been on a path of eroding the peace and hope of the world, both from economic standpoints and a lack of peaceful means of negotiations. We can and we must build a bridge of trust back to our own government. The leader of the free world must be redefined into one of caring and providing, not policing and enforcing.

Corporate America

The current corporate influences have deep hooks in both major parties of our government system. It not only has influence in terms of the money required for re-election of many of our government officials, but it also has influence over mass media and the biased information that reaches us. It is troubling when we want to believe in the concept of a functioning democracy and free speech when in reality it is those who have the financial influence that control the news we get and have such a strong influence over those elected to best serve the people. This seems to simply be the system that those elected fall almost immediately victim to as politicians try so desperately to get re-elected.

We are now under what some have described as a corporate regime, which is actually nothing new to the United States of America. The following are identified as related periods in history where corporations had great influence in our government.

Corporate Regime Timeline

1865-1901: First Corporate Regime (built by the robber barons)
1901-1921: Progressive Regime
                (led by trust-busting President Teddy Roosevelt)
1921-1933: Second Corporate Regime
                (led by President Warren Harding & Herbert Hoover)
1933-1980: New Deal Regime
                (designed by President Franklin Roosevelt)
1980 - Present: Third Corporate Regime
                (sponsored by global corporations and Presidents Ronald Reagan; George Bush, Sr.; Bill Clinton; George W. Bush; and Barack Obama)

Here is a synopsis of the corporate power influence that big money has in the world economic landscape. A total of 200 corporations, 82 of which are American, dominate the global economy, producing 27.5% of the world's total economic activity. Their combined sales are now greater than the combined economies of 196 countries in the world minus the biggest. These company incomes are greater than 18 times the combined annual income of the 1.2 billion people or nearly ¼ of the total world's population that currently live in "severe" poverty.

Like all of us as human beings, we want a good life for ourselves and to provide for our family's future. We all want to feel important, appreciated, and would like to make a meaningful contribution. However, many of us are stuck because of this economic system we live in, an economic system in which money dictates and we are forced to compete instead of contribute. These numbers translate to a huge chasm of inequality. The top three shareholders of Microsoft own more money than all six hundred million people in Africa combined.

The truth of big corporate influence is made clear when we look at the share of federal taxes paid. For the largest corporations, the amount paid has dropped from 23.2 % in 1960 to 11.4% in 1998. In 1998, Texaco, Chevron, PepsiCo, Enron, WorldCom, McKesson, and the world's biggest corporation, General Motors, paid no federal taxes at all, and it has not gotten any better since then. Corporate concerns have drafted more than 3,100 bills shaping our government to fit the best interest of their balance sheet. This does make sense when we come to understand that in this financial system we want our team to win, and our companies doing well translates into the quality of life for its members. But we must understand one thing about the entity of a corporation: at the heart of a corporation is interest in itself.

Our government has rewritten the Constitution to ensure that the rights and protections now cover corporations, which our founding fathers never intended. The Supreme Court has been extending constitutional protections under the 1st, 4th, 5th, 6th, 7th, and 14th Amendments, securing the corporate right to spend billions of dollars through political action committees ("soft money") on political campaigns and Washington lobbying, immune from public scrutiny. This has been the perfect breeding ground for savings and loan scandals that cost the public billions of dollars: Enron accounting scandals, Putnam mutual fund fraud, and Wall Street currency trading scandals just to name a few in our recent history. It is similar corruption that led to the implosion of the government system in the Soviet Union - not the Reagan policies that may have been publicized.

Here are a few examples of government talk for re-election vs. government action ability for the people as provided by our previous President, George W. Bush. It is an excellent example of what one needs to say to be elected versus what can be done due to the real world restrictions of our current economic system. What he said:

"I am touched by the kids, nurses and doctors, all of whom are working to save lives. I will make sure the health care systems are funded."

What he did: Bush's first budget proposed cutting funds to children's hospitals by 15% or $34 million.

His 2004 budget proposed cutting another 30% or $86 million from grants to children's hospital.

What he said: "We've got to do more to protect worker pensions."

What he did: Four months later, the Treasure Department proposed highly controversial rules that would allow employers to resume converting traditional pension plans to new "cash balance" plans that can lower benefits to long-serving workers. Critics say the rules violate federal law by discriminating against older workers.

What he said: "The most important issue for any governor in any state is to make sure every single child in your state receives a quality education."

What he did: His 2004 budget proposed to cut vocational and technical education grants by 24% or $307 million to provide a basic education to our children.

Compared to our economic system theories, our politics are no science, and only political scientists usually know that. The only science that is used is the science of re-elections. It is unfortunate that our elections simply patch up systems that continue to deteriorate our society, and to what end? We live in a frame work that unfortunately gives power to those who have the influence, and the influence comes with money, hence the power of corporate influence. What a sad truth it is that our economic system is based on a theory that is proven both false and true many times and that our politics are not based on a science at all.

This book and plan is not about thinking small. I It's all about moving the ball forward with clear and concise guidelines that are based on truths, trust, and the science of human nature. Not a set of proven and then disproven theories, but a tangible way of caring for each other aligned with how we are made by nature to receive what we truly desire. Most of that is to have our efforts be appreciated.

Something is wrong when war becomes a political platform. However in 2004, Karl Rove, a political advisor to George W. Bush, became laser focused on the virtues of war on terror and shoring up the GOP base while capturing suburban independents who might defect if the campaign focused on domestic concerns such as job creation, debt and fiscal responsibilities, environmental protections, social security, education, trade, corporate welfare and scandals, energy policy, global warming, and poverty and inequality. The corporate influence and scandals touch ever so close to the top levels of our government: Enron CEO Ken Lay contributed more to George W. Bush's lifetime career than any other funder. Previous Vice President Cheney's connection to Halliburton was well publicized, and the Iraq war proved to be a $17 billion client. We all but dismiss it as pro quo of our business climate. The fact is that relationships should have a lot to do with your business. Let's look at some of the historically positive influences government has made on our society. One example as possibly having the most profound effect, Theodore Roosevelt became the first president to launch a European-style social democracy in America, and his ideas saved capitalism. These "socialist" methods inspired some of the most important legislation of the 20th century. He was responsible for:

* Social Security Act

* Wagner Act (legalized unions and collective bargaining)

* Public Works Administration

* Emergency Relief Appropriations Act

(created big government programs to employ jobless worker)

* Glass Steagall Act (strictly regulated banking and Wall Street)

* Holding Company Act

(broke up utilities and other big holding companies)

* Rural Electrification Act (created public utilities)

The affluent attacked these ideas as socialism, but workers all over America found that politics finally meant something: a job, a voice, a little respect, in effect creating and protecting the American middle class. FDR did not approach leading America with small ideas, playing defense, or patching up systems. His ideas were bold, venturous, and revolutionary, and they had a profound effect on many generations that followed who now have come to rely on these programs.

Quality of Life

Within this chapter we look at current trends and shine the light on the subjective quality of life here as Americans. Do you rank transportation, medical care, GDP, cell phones or maybe flat screens per capita to help quantify or attach a figure to the quality of life? The International Living magazine answered that question this way – "No, you can't." How do we *measure* and what do we *measure* to quantify the quality of life and its current trends?

Much like a stock chart, we know that there are too many variables that could affect a quality of life measurement. Frankly it is too personal of a question to think in sweeping terms of a country. A 9.5% unemployment rate doesn't seem like a bad number until you lose your job. The quality of life is not the same as a standard of living, which is more materialistically measured. While possibly not on all accounts, in general our standard of living has continued to rise since the introduction of the automobile. We all seem to have microwaves, big screen TVs, and what American kid doesn't have some form of iPod? Buying all these foreign products might help with our standard of living index, but does it necessarily equate to a better quality of life? In terms of life quality, you need to be asking yourself some pretty simple questions. How is my health? How are my relationships with friends and family, or what am I doing to help others? This is where true quality of life is felt and defined as you feel a value in yourself.

How does the fact that we can't afford our own American products and service affect us? It starts by practically requiring two incomes to live the American Dream of owning a home and possibly retiring relatively financially secure for the 99% of us. Just as there is no denying the strain and deterioration of the family unit, which strikes to the very core of many ancillary issues, there is no denying the financial strain and requirements the economic system has put on us as Americans.

Billy Graham offered a prayer for our country shared on the famous Paul Harvey show. This drew more response than any other story in the history of his show that spanned more than four decades. This prayer helps put in perspective how we as Americans in a quest for more have lost touch with our values, and in turn, this quest of greed has aided in the deterioration of a quality of life or has put a further distance from what some might coin "the good ole' days." The days where family and community were more at the core of our being, and things were simpler and possibly even a little better. Here's the prayer from Billy Graham:

> *'Heavenly Father, we come before you today to ask your forgiveness and to seek your direction and guidance. We know Your Word says, 'Woe to those who call evil good,' but that is exactly what we have done. We have lost our spiritual equilibrium and reversed our values. We have exploited the poor and called it the lottery. We have rewarded laziness and called it welfare. We have killed our unborn and called it choice. We have shot abortionists and called it justifiable. We have neglected the discipline of our*

children and called it building self-esteem. We have abused power and called it politics. We have coveted our neighbor's possessions and called it ambition. We have polluted the air with profanity and pornography and called it freedom of expression. We have ridiculed the time-honored values of our forefathers and called it enlightenment. Search us, Oh God, and know our hearts today; cleanse us from every sin and Set us free. Amen!'

Reverend Billy Graham

If you believe in the Christian faith, we know that forgiveness is at the forefront, but this prayer simply sheds some light on the moral deterioration of our society.

Currently the deteriorating economy has shown us what kind of an effect the economic system can have on our quality of life. We have received not just glimpses of this, but we have felt snippets of what the quality of life must have felt like when the 1929 stock market crashed and the great depression swept our nation with the huge number of foreclosures and people being displaced from their homes having everything repossessed. The only difference is now it feels like the government pumped in $7 trillion dollars into our economy to save us, and we really got nothing for it beside a little time and false hope. Here are a few questions that come to mind when trying to measure the quality of life that we have come to expect as citizens of the United States.

* Are we appreciated at our work?
* Do we have ample time for quality vacations?
* Do we have sufficient quality time with our family?

71

* Are we connected with our community?

According to The Carrot Principle books, employee motivation statistic show that by far the greatest single contribution to productivity is appreciation and recognition for a job well done. Do we really need the statistic of 66% ranking it as the number one motivator of productivity, or is it something we all know inside? In study after study, appreciation outranks money as the motivator in the workplace. It is said that if a worker was not happy with the money they were getting, they would have left. But it is the day to day appreciation that makes one enjoy what they are doing. It is appreciation for one's work that gives us an immeasurable self-worth, and this is simple because it is within us all and at the essence of what we are trying to capture in this outlined path for real societal change.

When you look back at the moments you remember vividly, you can't help but remember the vacations shared with your family as part of those thoughts. For whatever reason, when we get away to explore new things and separate ourselves from the routine of life, those become the moments we remember. Unfortunately, it is no secret that Americans continually rank at the bottom of vacation time taken. We all wish there could be a better way, but know that we must accept it as it is. The quality time with our family and being connected with our community can bring true fulfillment. I think we all really realize that we get so much more back when we give, and it is up to us as individuals to make the effort while understanding that there are challenges. The plan outlined here is about giving more time back to the family and truly having an effect on that which is most important.

Societal Collapses

Considering the current set of economic circumstances, the question, "Can our society survive?" begs to be asked and acknowledged in a review of our current trends as Americans. Historically, there have been many more societal collapses than there have been wars. I believe we all could agree that there are many factors that could contribute to the collapse of a society: the environmental factors, the economic system, or a manmade war in which one country destroys another country's way of life. Beyond grading where ourselves against these factors, just let the notion of collapse resonate for a minute. Then we can take comfort in the resiliency of the human species. But as individuals united, we could change or create anything and change it very quickly.

Societies such as the ancient Mayans, the revered Roman Empire, the defeated German Regime, the war torn regions of Somalia and Rwanda, and the recent economic collapses of Russia, Iceland, Spain, and Portugal seem to be the coming of the tide. It should be noted that Russia was once considered a "super power," and Iceland was recently touted as having one of the thriving economies in the world. Societal collapses have occurred continually in the last 2000 or so years.

(Think about that for a second. We could almost think of that as 25-30 generations, which does not seem like that long ago when you start to think about how far you could go back with your own family.)

To clearly make the point, we need to acknowledge that we as an American society logically understand - we can feel and rightfully fear a complete economic collapse here in the United States. It is acknowledged that our current path is unsustainable. Considering that it is the American dollar that has come to the rescue of countries like Spain and Greece when they faced collapse, it is mind boggling to think what would happen if the economic system of the United States collapsed given that the entire world economic system is based on the dollar.

As an engine for the world economy, our severe deterioration is already being felt in many other countries. Our recession is their recession. To make mattesr worse, we can couple the economic effects on our society with the growing effects our changing environment has on our world. We saw the power of Katrina, and now we all have a little more fear that hurricane season may be living with a little more strength now. By watching my home town of Cedar Rapids, Iowa, become engulfed in eight feet of water, or seeing pictures and hearing accounts of the awesome power of the Indonesian tsunami, it becomes apparent that our environment can change in an instant. Not to detract from the fact that our environment can change over a slower period of time

74

where we continue to become acclimated to its changes, much like the boiled frog illustration.I That is, if a frog jumps into boiling water it will recognize that it is hot and immediately jump out, but if the water is slowly turned up, it will remain as it boils.

Are we simply acclimating to these changing environmental conditions, or will the harsh climate force us to finally change? Will we acclimate to the change in our economic condition, or will there be some sort of storm or man-made event that will act as the proverbial straw to our society?

I am here to say that there is a different way, a way in which we can live with love and trust for our neighbor and our own government. There is a method in which we can create a society where we can live with the confidence of knowing that, together, we have all the resources necessary to respond to any situation and to ensure that all of our citizens are safe and have the opportunities to connect and to thrive in a community where we all are accepted and appreciated.

Chapter 3 – Love and Altruism is the Answer

"Every person must decide whether to walk in the light of creative altruism or the darkness of selfishness. This is the judgment. Life's most persistent and urgent question is what are you doing for others?"

Rev. Dr. Martin Luther King

"Those that eat and do not contribute are stealing."

Mahatama K. Gandhi

"Only love can conquer hate"

Marvin Gaye

ALTRUISM DEFINED

Altruism is defined as an unselfish giving of oneself without regards to any reward for the giver. It can be displayed as a spirit in our concern for others or by our actions in the way we work, the way we help a family member, care for a baby, work as part of a PTA, bring cookies to a neighbor, help a perfect stranger stranded on the side of the road, or join a sandbag team to hold back the rising tide.

Van Gogh's – Parable of a Good Samaritan

The spirit of altruism is the heart and care we put into our work. It is rooted in the spirit of love, and it is within this spirit that we dream of a family and being part of a welcoming neighborhood and community. If led correctly, an entire nation could be rooted in this spirit of altruism. This book is about defining a clear road to change, changing our way of thinking and the systems we live in. We have the opportunity to root ourselves and our society in a spirit of altruism. What we are trying to do is move our society from one based in fear and competition to one based in love and appreciation.

Before we can do anything with this spirit, we need to understand its roots, its meaning, and the studies of how altruistic behavior works naturally within us. Regardless of the changes made, we can all agree that we would like a society that captures our natural tendencies and brings out the best in each of us. Let us let the spirit of love trump greed and competition in order to better serve each other. Conversely, egoism is the selfishness of doing for oneself even at the cost of others. Psychological egoism claims that each person has but one ultimate aim: his or her own welfare. Does this sound more like the norm of our current society? That is because systemically we live in world where there is fear for survival. We must all be guilty if we are to believe the immortal words of Dr. King: that injustice anywhere is a threat to justice everywhere. If we are serving injustice to each other anywhere, we end up serving it everywhere. But injustice has become engrained within the system in which we live.

Altruism is a traditional virtue in many cultures and at the core of religious traditions such as Judaism, Christianity, Islam, Buddhism, Confucianism, Sikhism, Hinduism, and Universism. As I open myself to understand religions, I see that at the core, people seek any of them to become better people and to find acceptance in something larger than themselves. In addition, altruism is a key aspect of many humanitarian and philanthropic causes, exemplified in leaders such as Dr. Martin Luther King, Jr., Gandhi, and Mother Teresa. This idea was often described as the "golden rule" of ethics. Through our own giving, we find a sense of self-actualization. Altruism as a mechanism for societal interaction takes place in many forms and many studies have been done regarding altruism. The issue of indebtedness is of particular interest because it speaks to the systemic changes described here. For most of us, when we have someone give to us, we naturally feel a sense of indebtedness, unless it is a child-parent relationship or our siblings. If we can capitalize on this indebtedness and somehow use this knowledge of our natural tendencies to give and reciprocate, then we can set up a societal structure that makes sense because it would incorporate our natural tendencies. We can capture this spirit and inject it into the systems by which we provide goods and services to each other and even as a part of our governance.

Conversely, war is not a method for true social change. Our great thinkers and leaders, such as Jesus, Plato, Gandhi, and Dr. King, all used the same power to influence real positive change. Their shared thinking was not to fight your enemy to conquer; they knew that this way of thinking will not make your enemy your ally. In theory, conquering for Americans never meant that we wanted to take over a country, but I wonder if there is a better way than simply trying to shoot each other to bring about peace and change. Do you wonder if "the enemy" (that boy with the gun) might be just like us? That if they could find a productive opportunity to provide for their families, secure a future, and bring honor to themselves and the association they are with, that they would choose a different profession than that of being a gun operator or a hired government assassin?

Dr. King studied under Professor George Davis, who emphasized the role of altruism in creating community. He indicated that this altruism of evangelicalism had led to the abolition of the slave trade in the British Empire and to many other philanthropic enterprises including prison reform, establishment of schools and orphanages, care of the poor, protection of children, relief for the mentally ill, and factory reform,. Furthermore, it was the basis for the reform of segregation in our country. Altruism promotes community. Professor Davis shared the vision of the beloved community. He maintained that, "For the sake of this community [of divine love], we lose ourselves and in it we become part of something much greater. I believe this is something we all long for."

As it has been said and understood globally, only love can conquer hate. So to understand the spirit of altruism, or the giving of love, we must explore love and its meanings. It is through the power and understanding of love that we can open ourselves up to new, basic societal fundamentals. Utilizing this power as a structure for our government and economic systems, we can transform not only our country but the entire world into a place of harmony and caring for our fellow man like never before in the history of mankind. Thanks to the discoveries, creative genius, and advancement we have made as a human race, the possibility is upon us.

The Greeks have three unique words for love. By understanding its different forms, we become more embracing of each other as a community; we become more embraced with love. These types of love are:

Agape – is an understanding, creative, redemptive goodwill towards all men. It enables us to love every man not because we like him or because his ways appeal to us, but because God loves him. It is the love of God operating in the human heart. This love is spontaneous and groundless in the sense that it is not motivated by any attractive quality in the object. Agape does not even use the idea of "love of thy neighbor to gain God's love." Jesus, said it so clearly with, "Love one another as I love you, so love one another, for if you only love those who love you, what reward is there in that?" Think for a second what type of person someone like this must be.

By becoming a caring member of society, you find that society cares for you, and your love is returned a hundred fold as the bible tells us. Let us not only take comfort in that, but understand that together we can create and become a part of a loving world.

Philia – is an intimate affection between friends. In this love, we love because we are loved. Living in a neighborhood or community where you are a welcomed member is a warm and wonderful place to be. Your contribution is appreciated and welcomed in such an environment. It is a safe place where you are free to be you and comfortable to make the contributions unique to your personality. This relates to what has been written as a depiction of Heaven. There is acceptance and non-judgment towards one another, thy kingdom come, thy will be done on earth as it is in Heaven. The power to build a loving community can be and is upon us.

Eros – is the romantic or aesthetic love that Plato presented in his dialogues as the yearning of the soul for the realm of the divine. Is there any greater love or greater gift than that of finding someone you know you want to be connected to for your entire life? Are we not happiest when we find someone that we truly have fallen in love with? Subsequently, are we not happy to simply see a couple in the state of Eros? There is a true romantic love in all of us, yearning for the prince or princess of our dreams. Finding that person who we truly love can, by itself, lead to fulfillment in our lives. The soul is given freedom when we give neighborly love, such as when we share the words of Jesus Christ: "If you love them that love you, what thanks have you, for even sinners love those that love them." If we can place the spirit of love for one another in our hearts and recognize the philosophy of love as part of our societal culture, we will open up a beautiful world that we can all appreciate. A world where we can be appreciated and be a welcomed member of the human family.

Love can take many forms:

Celebration – to remind us that life is a blessing. This includes being a part of the moment, whether sharing and celebrating a birthday or building a piece of furniture for others to enjoy. Also, putting our hearts into the moment can open us up to the celebration and reverence for life. Living life with a heart of celebration provides true enjoyment and pride in the experiences around you.

Compassion – when someone needs support, we give of ourselves and through our giving, we discover ourselves. Stooping down to help family, friends, or a neighbor in need, we find great rewards by the compassion we express. With a true sense of empathy, we feel each other's joy and we share in each other's pain. This compassion fosters a true sense of kindness towards each other and a real sense of community as we journey and learn during our time together on this planet.

Forgiveness – when someone is truly apologetic and has learned from their errors or mistakes, we as people need and desire to be forgiven and to be reconciled with the community or a loved one. How powerful an image of forgiveness it is to see Pope John Paul II visiting the inmate who had tried to shoot him only weeks before.

Forgiveness is not only powerfully articulated in the Lord's Prayer where we are told the Lord is merciful and gracious, but it is at the core of Christianity that we are forgiven and accepted as imperfect. Releasing another from the bondage of their sin or mistake creates a powerful sense of love, and we can give this acceptance to one another and to ourselves. Recognizing that we all have faults helps us in our confidence to take risks. That we all learn from our mistakes means that we in turn become better people. Why would we waste mistakes? Why would we as people not embrace someone's learning? Do we not allow our children as many attempts as they need to learn something new? How many times would we allow a child to fall before giving up on their ability to walk? By forgiving, we create a welcoming and caring society.

To illustrate this point, let's return to the way we drive. We spend thousands of hours driving and none of us expect each other to be perfect 100% of the time. As drivers, we all know that sometime within our lifetime we will likely be in an accident regardless of who is at fault. Obviously, we don't want this, but we allow ourselves to accept the possibility and try our best on the road. Every day we pass each other with only a couple of painted lines to separate the control of our cars moving past each other at a combined speed of up to 100 mph or more. When an accident does occur, our system requires that we instantly place blame so that we can review punitive damages, involve insurance companies, and try to avoid lawyers and lawsuits. If we look at others' mistakes as an opportunity to make them pay due compensation, we create a cold world and foster fear of not performing perfectly for fear of being sued, unappreciated, or fired.

In all forms of love we give of ourselves, and within our giving we find pride and discover the person we want to be. Plato accepted the belief of the Oriental doctrines of salvation: that the human soul has a supernatural divine origin and worth. He believed that the soul can experience Eros, or a true love for another human being. As a result the soul can ascend to the divine because this love is divine in origin. His theory states that prior to its involvement with the body, the soul had a vision of the divine. It could see the essences of Truth,

Goodness, and Beauty with the flaws that accompany their material manifestations. This divine love, the distinctive feature of freedom in giving, has its direct continuation in Christian neighborly love. Having received everything freely from God, one is prepared also to give freely. To do God's work, or that which you feel in your heart you are called to do, is the greatest calling and takes all forms in the way we give of ourselves for the betterment and service of others.

The 20th century's great altruism scientist Pitirim Sorokin led a Harvard research center in the study of creative altruism. In his study titled, "The Ways and Powers of Love," where he makes the point that we have studied the negative types of human beings sufficiently – the criminal, the insane, the sinning, and the selfish. However, we have neglected the creative genius, the saint, and the good neighbor. Around the time that the atomic bomb had been introduced, he concluded that what humanity needs is a quantum leap both in the understanding and implementation of creative altruism. This is a timeless need, and I hold that it remains true today as it has for the existence of humanity. There is a true sense of hope when we open ourselves up to the understanding of love and the power of good that exists within all of us in as many varying forms as there are individuals. Sir John Tempelton, a pioneer in the financial market and a knighted philanthropist, left a legacy of continued funding and research of natural sciences and theology upstanding character. He suggested that love is not a creation of people but rather people are a creation of love.

With this, he reminds us to be open to the compounding effects of love and appreciation for each other. Through our caring actions, we have a universal impact that spreads in the same way we see negative sentiments work within our history, possibly with an even greater power because powerful sentiments of love are appreciated. As compared to negative sentiments, which often lead to people turning their heads.

MECHANISMS DEFINED

The source of altruism is a natural quality that exists in all humans in varying degrees. Scientifically identifying the source of such unselfish behavior, it could be considered one or more parts of the following: (1) it is in our DNA and literally hardwired into our physiology; (2) altruism is part of natural law as an accepted and fostered community member and; (3) it is a major component of the drive for social behavior as we are drawn to it in an effort to be part of a community.

HOW

Very few species outside of humans practice altruism outside of their family circle. This puzzles scientists because it doesn't provide immediate benefit or personal gain – seemingly reducing the altruist's chance for survival. There are many studies and many philosophies going back to 1859 where Darwin wrote plainly in his study, "On the

Origin of the Species" that a tribe that collaborated would be victorious over most other tribes. Relate this collaboration theory to society as a whole, and we start to form the question of which would a society be better served by competition or collaboration? Or applied in theory, if a pile of sand needs to be moved, would it be better to argue over who can do it more efficiently and then allow the one that wins to do it, or if both are willing to help to simply allow them to work together?

The study of why people act in an altruistic way goes back to many great philosophers in written history; Aristotle believed that all humans were inherently good but that their potential could be realized only within society. Did he mean that if we lived within the isolation of the woods that we might not reach our potential? That we make a life by what we give? He went on to refer to our species as zoon politikon, the political animal. When Aristotle called man a political animal, he did not have parties and elections in mind. Man is a *zoon politikon* in the sense that the *polis*, the "city-state," is the natural culmination of man's nature; it is his end, as far as social organization goes. Not that all men live in cities. First comes the family, which arises out of biological necessity; next the tribal village in which man may more easily obtain the necessities of life than in the family alone. The city may come into being thereafter, so that man may pursue, in leisure, his highest nature. As Aristotle says in the beginning of his *Politics*, "Every city is a kind of association, and every association is joined together for the sake of some good." It is a very interesting note that the early political basis had the community in mind and at the basis of politics, from there we are joined for a greater good, possibly on to the county, state, and federal levels all being connected for the greater good.

It is our competitive marketplace that has left a trail of failed businesses (for many who simply desired to serve the greater good). It is the capitalistic system that does not work and flow with our natural tendencies for collaboration of the greater good. Eighteenth century thinker and French-Swiss philosopher Jean-Jacques Rousseau proposed in the novel *Emile* that the key to happiness was the free development of each child's personality. If we are to believe that we were all born with a gift and true happiness comes from sharing that gift and having it appreciated, that is aligned with our hope and desire we have as parents and the wonderment of what a new child can bring to the world. If we are free to raise our children with the goal of bringing out that which is in them to contribute, and our society helps by the structure and systems which are designed to support that in all human beings, then we have the basis for a harmonious society. This society is extremely different from that which we currently live in (a society of competition rather than collaboration).

Unfortunately, our current reality is that the desire to use our "gift" as a method of contribution is either met with unfettered determination by the child, or it is truly fostered by the nurture of the parents, or the notion is squashed by the needs for survival within the structure of the family or societal circumstances. The goal here is to open our eyes to the possibility of creating systems and a structure to society that truly supports and appreciates everyone's unique gifts and what good they can offer the world.

In 1976, the British evolutionary biologist Richard Dawkins reopened the study of altruism with his best-selling novel *The Selfish Gene*. In this novel, he describes our selfishness or unselfishness at the molecular or gene level. He provided the socio-biological theory of reciprocal altruism. People are most likely to help one another if frequent contact is expected in the future, or a relationship with the understanding: "I'll scratch your back if you scratch mine." The giver assumes that his/her generosity will be reciprocated at a later date. It is this notion, this natural tendency, that we are trying to capture here in this proposed change to our economic system where we give because it is good for mankind. Recent studies have been made of altruism, testing individuals for the amount they were willing to give.

- The results showed that 20% were willing to give if there was no punishment for not giving and if the subject did not know the other participants.
- The percentage jumped to 55% if there was a punishment for not giving.

- The giving increased to over 90% if there was a punishment and the giver knew the participants and that there would be reciprocation.

Imagine that social acceptability was a part of the influence and you knew that your giving was to be reciprocated.

These studies show and confirm our natural tendencies that lead us to give far more if we know that there are ramifications for no giving. Additionally, they prove that our giving will be reciprocated, which supports the change proposed here. This is an absolute key point to the proposal for a new economic system.

Capturing our innate desires to give and to be appreciated and using that as the basis for an economic system provides a platform for unlimited possibilities. Time has come for us to unite for change, to organize and eliminate "cuts" to our budget, cuts to social programs, cuts to our security and needed medicine. These are the programs that we have come to appreciate, such as safety and protection, our children's education, Medicare, roads, and other general social and welfare programs. Let us give each other a place within our society where we can create or be a part of providing services or the making of goods that serve mankind. Let's give each other the chance to enjoy and appreciate the gifts and talents we share.

Let's give way to the fear that work - any work - is below us. As a community, let's give our farmers the assurance that they can count on us if they need help when it is time for harvest. Let us not fear that the crops won't be picked or the bathroom won't be cleaned, after all we are the 99% who have cleaned our own bathrooms.

Genes / Human Nature

In human beings, the infant's protracted dependency, the dawning consciousness, and possibly general cuteness open up a narrow evolutionary window for tender altruistic sentiments and unselfish ends towards another human. Cognizant and acute awareness of this feeling and applying this compassion to the race of mankind is powerful. It opens us up to become a caring, welcoming, and compassionate community. The poetic words sung by the late Jim Croce put our current state into context: "You say you love the baby, but you crucify the man." If we can somehow capture the love we have when we see a baby and apply that which we feel in our heart, it opens ourselves up to an agape type of love in a community where all of us are accepted and where we can all be appreciated. Innumerable everyday people excel in loving-kindness, not just for family of nearest and dearest but as a volunteer on behalf of the neediest. Generous love for others is where we find purpose in our life, the most enduring source of meaning and dignity, and the basis for an all lasting self-esteem. The alternative to growth in love includes a drifting malaise devoid of purpose and accomplishment, the sense of "just hanging out," or that "same old shit, different day" sentiment I have heard far too often. The giving of oneself for the betterment of others always gives one an elevated sense of purpose, creative endeavor, and our own well-being. Altruism flows from a sense of self and is shared as a part of all humanity.

Human nature is malleable and our society has shown it through the acceptance of propaganda in our patriotic thinking. We are also malleable in positive ways, such as our changed acceptance of smoking in public places or drunk driving. I would argue that it is our social acceptability that has a far greater influence on our actions than any law.

We have seen the malleability of human nature work conversely as a negative influence in many forms. This includes the drug use and peer pressure that our adolescents face. Likewise, our support of war shows our willingness to be "sold" on the argument that there's a necessity to bomb our world neighbors. We'd choose to fight versus having the leaders of nations reaching out to sit down at the table of discussion and understanding.

Within this proposal for social change, I hope that we recognize how our malleability and the rule of social acceptance creates change. I believe the "laws" of simple social acceptance are much more powerful than laws or regulations. We can use this understanding as a cornerstone of confidence that we as a people will shape what is right and what is acceptable in a society that has changed. That does not mean that laws aren't necessary. This country was built on laws, and it also is a cornerstone of our society defining clearly what is right and acceptable.

EXCEPTIONS

In contrast to acceptance, today's American society fosters a sense of blame. Recognizing that there is a fine line between accountability and blame, let's look at a few examples on the way we look for the person responsible in an auto accident or hold judgment and liability because the coffee is too hot or the sidewalk too slippery.

We should be finding acceptance and recognizing that accidents simply happen to all of us, that none of us are perfect 100% of the time, and that we can use these types of incidents to learn. Instead, in our modern day, some people use these opportunities in an attempt to hit their own personal lottery by suing and blaming. Some try to take advantage of such situations out of the fear that they won't be cared for, either in regards to their injury, never winning the lottery, or not being able to take care of their families. I would be so bold to say that if all of your needs were met, if you were a millionaire for example, and you broke your leg on a slippery floor, you would take care of your leg and not look for blame and retribution. It is when fear replaces love that we begin to think about the requirements of surviving. That's when the spirit of altruism is taken over by that of an egoist, and we begin to act in a selfish manner because we are concerned for our own well-being. It only seems natural that if our survival needs are already met we will be in a position to want and desire to give of ourselves more for the betterment of others, the road that brings us all closer to self-actualization.

Christianity introduces us in the image of God, but marred by the failure of sin. There is a point in that which we can all agree that none of us are without fault. There may be only a few that ever lived on this Earth that have ever come close to perfection through their way of living by a loving and giving heart. . By accepting the imperfection in ourselves, it gives us all a common bond and helps us to better accept it in others Within this acceptance, we give each other a safe place to succeed or fail. Recognizing that failure becomes a part of our learning landscape, we must fail if we are to succeed – look at the invention of the light bulb for instance.

Our acceptance changes our society from one that takes advantages of fault (which we all have), to a place where we can accept and appreciate one another's best efforts. All we can hope for is someone's best effort. In a roundabout way, this is connected to feedback given from the General's observation in Iraq. The General suggested that there is far less violence when there is work and the means for people to provide for their families. Our inner desires are met when we are given the opportunity to succeed and productively contribute as a valued member of our community. It is sad to think that there are simply not enough opportunities because of the limits our economy poses on us or that every town could not have a new plant that employs 10,000 people. It is sad that we cannot live in a world where we concentrate on providing for everyone instead of living in fear that our circumstances may change.

Living in Seattle, we felt that our community had lost the big game, and in the back of our mind had the twinge of fear of recession when we learned that Boeing was not putting their new airplane plant here but in Charleston, SC. As any city would be, Charleston was ecstatic with the new opportunities that were not there before - everyone with resounding sense of cheer.

Factories closing and the lack of opportunities within a community creates fear and instability. We see a rise in crime, drug use, and violence in our inner cities. Where there are many opportunities we see often see a growing community. Making a valued contribution, whether it's helping with canned corn, building cars, or silicon chips, being a part of an organization, especially one that serves others, gives us a sense of worth and builds community and appreciation for one another. The lack of opportunities works in reverse. There are far more people ready to work than the system and the restrictions of the monetary system allow. This a worldwide problem.

Seventeenth century English philosopher Thomas Hobbes considered that humans are a species of wild animals that constantly oppress our own kind. Our instinct for self-preservation expresses itself in an unquenchable lust for power. This would inevitably result in a battle of all against all if not for the presence of a king who made social cohesion within a state possible. Stating the obvious we need leadership, and we need a shared vision. a direction that we can believe in as it unites us. We need leaders who will stand up and speak of their vision, which hopefully will be good, and those who speak to the people that believe in the same direction becomes the voice of the people.

This type of thinking may also hold the secret to world peace. If, for instance, we used the United Nations as an inclusive place where we could try to work together as one world, then one king overseeing The United Nations of Earth could unite us all. This would be someone that each of our world leaders reports to when it comes to world affairs; someone who fosters cooperation between nations so that it will best serve the human race; someone who can bring an end to wars.

Conflicted Study

There are those who are convinced that no matter how genuine our love for others might appear, in reality human beings are only capable of selfish motivations. In today's society, it has been stated that altruism is grounded in self-interest and reputational investment. It has been theorized that the secret of the Good Samaritan is that his or her altruistic act would be discerned and publically acknowledged. I would contend that it is true that when you help another it becomes a sense of pride, and we do want to share this story with our spouses or others, but of course doing good is something we want to share.

There comes a point where efforts to explain away such extensive love rather than accept it at face value approaches absurdity. It has been said, "Scratch an egoist and watch an altruist bleed." When you think about someone being selfish when they receive care from others, that natural tendency to reciprocate provides a fuel for a social indebtedness, and we will see the natural altruistic behavior in any human being. Capturing this fuel of social indebtedness and reciprocation is at the heart of the social changed detailed here. We can use this to start a wildfire of love and acceptance that grows and burns brightly in the most beautiful way all across America and the world. Within us all is our desire to help another, to have our work and our person appreciated. For example, Mother Teresa was good regardless of what came out in the latest biographical journals. I believe there is a little of Mother Theresa in all of us, just like our makeup contains some of the traits we admire in every person that walks the planet. By being the person you are, the qualities you have observed and incorporated are those you have witnessed in other people, whether we are conscious of this or not. We admire her because her acts of kindness remind us that we are all indeed kind and that we all would hope that someone loves us when we are in need.

It could be argued or theorized that genuine altruistic traits give way to greed, as we see on Wall Street where it is all about serving the dollar. When events such that happened on 9/11/01 or hurricane Katrina, we realize that love for fellow human kind exists innately within us all. This love simply gets suppressed within our self. The willingness to help has never been stronger, and we want our giving to have more meaning than simply writing to the latest charitable cause with a wonder and hope of where are giving really goes. When given the choice to help in a sandbag chain to prepare for an impending flood or hang out at home, we find ourselves fulfilled with the sense of participation in community. When we make ourselves a part of the choir and become part of the song sung by many, we realize that it is beautiful music that we can all take pride in.

MECHANISMS

We are natural-born reciprocators; the great majority of our relationships are based around reciprocation. Becoming the recipient of an altruistic effort in turn makes us want to do the same for others. It is a part of our natural tendencies. I can remember being stranded with a car that would not start. I was in desperate need of someone who not only was willing to give my car a jump, but also had the jumper cables necessary to do it. That kind person was sent from Heaven. Returning to her car with Starbucks coffee in hand, she rescued me with her car and her cables. With a new found sense of gratefulness, I in turn wanted to find fifty people that needed similar rescuing. It is the sense of reciprocation that has the power to exponentially grow an altruistic society with a much greater motivation than money can ever provide.

A sense of altruism opens us up to a new freedom and unrestricted possibilities within our community. It is not simply our receipt of such altruistic behavior, it is also our witness to it that has an effect and fuels our desire to give.

The lessons we learn:

A story of a race from a recent Special Olympics event: a girl had fallen behind the group of racers and struggled to make it around the track. As the leader was about to cross the finish line, she looked back and noticed the lagging racer. Without hesitation, the leader turned around, and as she did, the entire group followed and ran back to gather the straggler. All the racers surrounded and encouraged the struggling girl to finish the race. As they all crossed the finish line together, they were greeted with a standing ovation from a crowd who truly appreciated a raw, unselfish act.

This caring and sacrifice of one human being for another human being touches our hearts because the desire for us to care is within us all. Who was the winner and who was the loser in the race? We as society embrace unselfish acts. We encourage them, and when the opportunity is given, we want to be a part of giving to others.

In another story, a group of people over 80 years olds that volunteer for different causes, such as Meals on Wheels and Rocking Neglected Babies, were asked of their attitude towards helping people. All of their responses held a common thread, and when we look inside, I believe we can all relate to their sentiment, "It's an honor to help other people, because we are all really the same," and "Everyone should help out in their community — how else will things get done?" When asked, they all speak of the gifts they receive by giving of themselves — not what they are giving.

It is amazing that we are created in a way that we feel a gift of self-worth when we ourselves give.

Social Darwinism studied the "survival of the fittest," and it has become a term synonymous with success in the United States. This concept has justified the struggle of winners and losers in our society and has promoted extreme inequality. This current business climate has resulted in a plummet of the "working class" from 40% in the 1950s to our current 23% in an industrialized area such as Seattle.

Altruism always requires setting aside the self as the center of the universe and taking up a fundamental orientation toward others. Peter Kropotkin, the 18th century Russian-born philosopher and studier of human tendencies, discovered this when he was introduced to workers in Switzerland, most of whom were watchmakers. The isolated and self-sufficient nature of the workers impressed Peter. He saw a community of workers that succeeded when permitted to work according to their own interests but bound by a common goal and supervised direction. He introduced the study of socialism into Russia and stated that the real principle of morality is defined as the higher concept of not taking revenge for wrongs and of freely giving more than one expects to receive from his neighbors. With that stated, I believe that not all of socialism, communism, or a democracy are evil. When we look, we find some good and bad in all these systems. With an understanding of human nature and a study of governments and economies around the world, the United States as a free nation and government run by the people can create a hybrid of many philosophies.

Creating systemic changes to our government and economy, we can capture our natural tendency to give and reciprocate the gifts of others.

Sooner or later, all the people of the world will have to discover a way to live together in peace, and thereby transform this pending cosmic elegy into a creative psalm of brotherhood. If this is to be achieved, man must evolve. For all human conflict is a method which rejects revenge, aggression and retaliation. The foundation of such a method is love.

Dr. Martin Luther King jr

Family

Babies take their mothers' beneficence for granted, and they do not have to buy it with acts of kindness. Brothers and sisters do not feel the need to reciprocate every kind act between each other. Conversely, unrelated individuals are acutely aware of social debts. This may be the reason I wanted to find and help 50 stranded motorists after I myself was aided.

When we look at how the spirit of altruism grows and how the expansion exists throughout a community or nation, we can easily realize that this happens through a variety of influences:

- survival needs of the larger group
- influence of culture
- moral logic of human equality
- influence of religious and ethical wisdom
- direct power of unlimited love
- simply being a witness to the action

SUMMARY

"Loving thy neighbor as thyself" is simple to say, and it lends us to a strong sense of community. Through your giving so shall you feel connected to those around you. However, our current era is leaving us with a lack of pride and sense of community. Simply getting a smile from our neighbor seems like a rarity these days in some parts of the country.

Altruism can be the catalyst for the change we seek in our country. If we understand the meaning of altruism and are given the opportunity and freedom to display our innate desire to be altruistic, our natural tendency to give, then we will all find ourselves with purpose. Additionally, we can all find our true self, and we will become a part of a caring, loving, and accepting community. If we can answer the following question in the affirmative, the door to all possibilities opens. "Does our current liberties and freedoms allow us to change our way of taking care of our people?" It is through our understanding of love that has given us the power to change our enemies into allies. In this case, it is not our enemies, but it is our own county's citizens, it is our American brothers and sisters that we which to make our allies through altruism. How do our complex brains, unique imaginations, communicative abilities, reasoning powers, moral sense, and spiritual promptings give rise to the remarkable and common practice of unselfish love? An unselfish love for our neighbors or for those we may not even know yet? If this question could be answered and the power of love be harnessed, the world would erupt into a community of not just hope but of real fellowship.

If we are to have a human future at all, it can only emerge from a love for humanity that transcends self, kind, and group to embrace everyone. As sung by the socially insightful Marvin Gaye, "Only love can conquer hate." We have seen it work with the non-violent approaches of Gandhi and Dr. King. This expansion defines both the moral and the spiritual points of view as bequeathed to us from all those perennial minds deemed wise in one tradition or another. The restructuring of the system proposed within this book harnesses this power, and the natural desire that is within us all.

It is through a sense of altruism that we weave a fabric of community and create a society that we can all take pleasure in being a part of. Waking up to a caring world that accepts, makes way, and appreciates what you and I have to offer. It changes a society where there are victims of competition to one where there are opportunities and welcoming sentiments all around us. This is the road to a social change that we all long for, but we have not been presented the idea of how we could possibly make it happen. Welcome to the possibility of a new world order.

Chapter 4 The Solution.

"85% of all quality problems are system related
and we have a natural inclination to do a good job."

Japan's Quality Guru
William Deming

Introduction

We have looked at the economic and political problems of our society, and now comes the time to provide a detailed road map to a complete solution. Within this chapter are the details of exactly how we can (1) build a bridge of trust back to our own government and (2) provide a method of solving the problems associated with our current economic system.

We have analyzed the many problems that we live with, and we have reviewed the current path of our society in previous chapters. Some of these problems have created a huge burden on us, our children, the following generations for the next 100 years, and also our parents that we are destined to care for. Our economy, the trust we have in our government, and our general trust for one another as members of the world family seems to have spiraled out of control. We continue to borrow against our future, and frankly, we grow more and more scared of what the future might look like for our economy. We have a hard time understanding and having hope considering what is actually upon us and the direction our government/nation is taking.

The founding fathers of our country worked to create a government that would serve democracy with the intent that it be reinvented for the needs of the people. Unfortunately, what we have seen is our government reshaped by corporate influences. It is our system of government, the influence of big money, what seems like endless bickering, and simply working within a system that feels broken that has led us to a path of mistrust, fear, and an uncertain economic future. The truth is that none of us have the confidence that any one person or any one vote can make a difference within the existing system of government. This lack of confidence is increased by the constraints our current economic system places on our government's ability to be truly effective and efficient.

Is there a reason that everyone in our society is not entitled to a dignified quality of life? Should a good education, a place to live, food, water, heat, and healthcare be a right or a privilege in a society such as ours?

The United States of America is not the same country it was 200 years ago. We have a lot to be proud of as a nation, and of course, we want to be proud of our heritage. Unfortunately, our history books are time-lined with wars and marked with recessions and depressions. Here and now, we have the opportunity to open the doors to embrace our advances and our instinctual gift of giving. To meet this instinct, we must give of ourselves for others, and in this way we can create a nation that lives in harmony and has a profound effect on the entire world. With our technology, training programs, opportunities, and our indomitable spirit, we can be confident that our country contains enough bravery to keep ourselves safe from aggression. Together we possess the muscle required to build the roads and bridges that are necessary to move our country forward. With love in our hearts, we can change the minds of our "enemy" when we are willing to sit down and discuss our differences to learn who they are, understand and help them address their struggles, and work in an effort to come to peaceful terms. The time is now; we have been crying out for real change election after election with candidates that can promise change but cannot deliver the change we desire.

A "clear" presented in the controversial book by L. Ron Hubbard titlted *Dianetics* describes a state of mind formed the basis for the Scientology religion. This enlightenment is described similarly in Buddhism, Hindu, and even Christianity (where we try to act the way Jesus would). This type of mindset opens our heart to make decisions that are above and free of social restraint so that we can dream and create in a society where all things are possible.

This is a clear approach to rebuilding our society in a manner more aligned with how we are made as people. Yes, we can create a society in which we work together in collaboration rather than competition.

Yes, we can create a system and society in which our efforts are valued and appreciated. Yes, we can create thriving communities where we are a welcomed part regardless if you live in a small town or big city.

As people of the world, we are characterized by our technological expertise and our capacity for mass production. The efficiencies of our communication system allows us to share information on an unprecedented scale, reshaping the landscape of our productivity. If we are honest, we are scared of what it has done to our society because within the current economic system our efficiencies seem to be working against us. Our technology and world economy has created growing efficiency and hyper-competitive marketplace where jobs, companies, and we as contributors are not in a place of instability. These changes proposed are about embracing these efficiencies and giving back to what is most important.

Imagine for a minute that your voice and ideas are not only welcomed but being given real consideration within your community and government. Imagine for a minute that roadway construction or the ability to build a park made possible by the will of the people and budgets surpluses if you will. Where the only deciding factors on moving forward with a project are, "Does it make sense to the community?" and, "Do we have enough willing participants and material resources available to make it happen?"

It's almost ironic that we all hope for economic salvation. We have all but lost hope that it is possible to elect a government that the American society can actually trust. Through that which plagues our society, I believe we all have come to understand that one politician or any one bill passed through Congress is not going to be able to correct the troublesome course we are currently headed down. The truth is that we as the people are the hope for the change we so desperately need in our country and all around the world. It takes something at the grass roots level to begin this change.

These changes to our systems and constructs begin with a belief that a plan can be created from a love for all mankind combined with a trust in your fellow man. This trust comes from the fact that we are really more alike than different and that we all share the same feelings and emotions. I want you to open yourself up to possibilities of real change as a united people. Using the methods built within our system of government, the structure is designed *for the people* that it serves to create a real systemic change when they are warranted. Change has been warranted for some time now.

We are the generation to create that change. The time is now, and we can stop hoping that our children will fix it all, or worse, have to pay for the debt we created. This is a take back-our-country, empower-the-people, revolution message. This book details a plan to modify our government system and a means of creating an economic system that works on trust and appreciation for one another.

How

We the people of the United States have this ability to create a societal systemic change not simply based on text book capitalism, or what we understand as communism, or even a socialist society. Instead, our ability is something aligned with altruism – a giving of oneself for the benefit of others. I'm talking about a system that is based on love, appreciation, and providing a structure to promote these for everyone. Within this structure, we grow in our connection as a community.

This solution is about harnessing the power of the people and trusting ourselves as individuals. It is undeniable that we want to care for our families and make a valuable contribution to society. Within a controlled and documented form of altruism and a *truly* democratic society where you have a voice, we can do just that.

Using much of the structures that are currently in place, many systems and organizations have been created, improved, and perfected throughout the years (i.e. City Council, Mayor, County jurisdiction, State Governor, etc.). Uniting these resources with our Senate and Federal resources, we all become part of one nation without taking away an identify of communities (i.e. New Orleans or San Francisco). It is time that politicians really became the public servants that they say they are, and then we can recognize and appreciate their contribution to our communities. This means all of us working together to help create a country with a shared view of our President, our state, and our local leaders. The true power lies within recognizing our similarities, realizing we are all much more alike than different, and knowing that we as the people have power if we all truly vote our conscience and are united as a people with a common goal.

Much like complaining about bad drivers but not really knowing anyone around you that you would consider one, we must trust ourselves and trust that the other person will take care of him or herself. Just like you we are all conscious beings. The power to really bring on change is in our ability to let go of fear and vote your own conscience, your vote and your support must be free from what the other guy may or may not do. Let us remember the truth: when the waters rise, we are amazed at all the people who come together to help stack sandbags and to protect against the possibility of flooding. We all are such willing to help.

Our government structure was designed to reinvent itself based on the needs of its people. We have come a long way in 230 years, and our government has not made but minor revisions to our government and economic systems. The greatest revision being the freeing of slaves, giving every man and woman the ability to vote, prohibition, the appeal of prohibition, and recently, corporations given citizenship rights and unbridled government influence. We, as the people, can make systemic changes that make sense for our current times, our societal advances, and the technology that can truly help with our efficiencies.

The solution outlined here embraces the voting process; the voice of the people; and the success and comfort we have within our democracy to create a United States government based on much of the structure we have in-place while utilizing the technology that has come to revolutionize the way we communicate.

It is a common understanding that if we choose to unite behind a plan, we the people can change anything. But we must also understand that change takes courage; it takes hope and confidence, and it takes trust in each other. The courage to become part of a revolution for our democratic liberty, and the courage for which I speak is by simply voting your own clear conscience, putting your name to a petition, or helping to organize. Let us all take a collective deep breath and realize that change can be accomplished if we can agree on a plan and accept the fact that it is possible because we as a people are choosing it to be.

Having the opportunity to really and truly create a piece of legislation detailing real change is what is being proposed here. We aim to petition each of our state governments, to call on an Article V Convention where we draft legislation for the American people to ratify three amendments to our Constitution. If ratified by 75% of the people's vote, this will effectively modify the structure to both our government and economic systems. It is time we do away with more cuts to our programs and start working on an expansion of services and a better lifestyle that affords us more quality time with our close friends and family while simultaneously allowing our creative gifts a greater chance to be given on the path to building and being a part of a growing community.

In addition to the proposed modifications on our governmental structure, we need a central data system that provides for an economic system based on something other than theories. This central data allows for complete cooperation between different governmental branches and agencies. It is time for us to create a system that does away with waste, duplication and triplication, and actually allows us to communicate. A closer integration from the federal to the local level will allow for cooperation and shared resources. Where thinking nationally, even globally, and acting locally truly mean something.

This is a proposal for using our system of democracy to restructure our economic system. We begin by clearing our minds and opening ourselves up to new possibilities. We continue by letting go of the fears that plague our culture's way of thinking: that there is not enough to go around. We must know that we live in abundance. We must stop worrying that someone might not pull his or her fair share when the truth is we all just want to help. Let go of the fear that you cannot find the person you'd need to barter with and/or fear that a change to our economic system would have to be some form of communism or socialism. When we start to question something new in the way of social systems, let's begin by asking the question: does anyone take advantage of the existing system or if we were to design something from scratch would this be what we design, especially with the facts we have? Are there trust babies who don't pull their fair share? The system proposed here demands fairness by the citizens that serve it and by virtue of its structure the system truly serves its citizens. This appreciation and trust for one another provides the basis for real change. The only question you should really be asking is "am I willing to contribute?" With opportunities everywhere, are you willing to help?

Additionally, it is far too easy to say that "someone" may take advantage of the system and not think in terms of what we as individuals might do to help. It is much like complaining about that bad driver but have difficulty naming more than 3 names. I wonder if anyone think that our current economic system lends itself to an unfair distribution. Does someone like Paris Hilton deserve much more than any of us just because of what her grandfather did? Under the proposed economic system, we can regulate ourselves and each other. This proposed system is based on the timeless words, "Ask not what your country can do for you, ask what you can do for your country." You will be needed; you will be asked to help, and it is everyone's desire that you participate. It is time we lived and experienced the abundance around us, not the limits and the budget cuts that plague our country and that continue to contribute to a world of ever increasing poverty and a widening the chasm of haves and have-nots that must stop.

So here is a solution that must be unveiled with the notion that we can trust each other. We must recognize that we are all more alike than different, that we as parents and children all want to be successful, and at the core of all of us, we have a need and desire to be appreciated. Let us embrace the notion that, on some level, we are all brothers and sisters, that evil does not lurk around every corner, that we can build a world of community, and we can work together to provide for each other. Let us let go of the discord, fear, and jealousies, and rather let us embrace and enjoy the abundance that surrounds us and do away with the current climate of never ending cuts and fiscal cliffs.

Let us change our fears that we are subject to the wind of the next round of layoffs into a certainty that our work and contributions are appreciated and needed. The fact is as a society we should all take great pride in the fact that we have succeeded in putting together the necessary infrastructure to allow a change like this to happen. Reviewing the studies of altruism, it is well documented that we are all much more willing to give of ourselves if we know that we can expect something in-return. It's such a simple truth. This proposed system harnesses that power, the power of that desire that our work be appreciated, our desire to give, and the simple truths that make us up as people. This innate desire to give of ourselves, reciprocation, and a sense of appreciation opens the door to true societal change and a new economic system more aligned with our actual human makeup.

The power of love is the only thing that can truly conquer hate and fear. And it is fear that we have within our current economic system. We must foster a society based on trust and truly build a community in which we are a welcomed member. To do this, we must make systemic changes to both the government and economic systems under which we as Americans now live. Only by making real systemic changes will this occur.

Think about this for a second. When you do anything based on fear versus doing that same thing with love and trust, what are the differences of the outcome or simply the way you approach any given effort? The fact is that this fear translates to a fear of survival and has transpired itself into greed and corruption at all levels. In anything we do out of fear, we not only set ourselves up for emotional pain but eventually failure because it cannot be sustained. So the challenge before us is to try to replace our failing economic system with one that promotes truths, not theories, trust not distrust, and appreciation for one another rather than greed.

Let's continue by establishing a baseline trust for one another. Look around you and remember that your life is, in a sense, held in the hands of nearly every adult around you. We already require each other's confidence and trust. We must trust each other's abilities to make split second timely taps of the toe or an ever so perfect slight movement of the hand as we pass each other daily, typically at a collective speed of well over 100 mph separated by nothing more than a couple of yellow painted lines on the road. – we must trust everyone if we are going to feel safe going anywhere that we won't cross that line, without this trust for one another we would be immobilized. In addition we must accept the fact that accidents happen and collectively we all are trying to avoid them to the best of our ability and giving our best is all we can expect of each other and that best is good enough.

President Obama stated boldly in his initial campaign that he would be willing to sit down and talk with leaders of Iran or other emboldened states, and for that he stood up to plenty of criticism. Our statements for American peace have been stated so well in the timeless words of John F. Kennedy: "Let us never negotiate out of fear, but let us never fear to negotiate." To sit down at the table with our potential enemies and extending a hand of friendship with a willingness to help seems to make more sense than punishing or shooting does. Of course we are willing to fight for love and peace, but that should mean at all levels, not just putting our young men and women in harm's way. It is the difference between love versus fear.

What we are talking about is not socialism, not communism, not even capitalism. What we are talking about is an accounted altruism under a democratic means of government. This proposed economic system captures our innate desire to give from the heart, and it works to fill our need to be appreciated and feel like that which is given is reciprocated. This is the basis for an economic system that opens the door to all possibilities fostering a community based on trust, brotherhood, and appreciation for each other.

Our Government

First thing in embracing a true systemic change in our government is that we must embrace the notion of a government For the People, By the People. Second we must realize that our Constitution was never meant to be eternal and unchanging. It was written by men and is intended for us as citizens of the United States to change it for the times. It only has value if we agree that the contents in the document provide the systemic framework that is best for our country. Not only is it within our rights to amend it as citizens, but it is also within the intentions of those that authored the document that it be changed when needed. There are many things about our government that work; there are many systems of public management and programs designed for communities at the City, County, State, and Federal levels that have been put into place that are designed to serve in a positive manner. Unfortunately, the system of priority influence combined with our economic system and plummeting budget constraints are deteriorating our government's ability to serve.

We are proposing two modifications to the structure of our Federal Government structure in addition to the change in our economic system. These modifications will be made possible thanks to the advances in our communication systems and a trust that we have for each other as responsible citizens. With the two amendments to our Constitution we accomplish our goal of building a bridge of trust from our people back to our own government, to make our government a partner of the people and give ourselves as American citizens a true voice.

Electoral College

As mentioned, the systemic changes we propose are a dynamic shift from a system based on fear to a system based on trust. The Electoral College was created in fear that we as the people could not be trusted with the ability to use our vote wisely to elect a President. The notion was that we may be susceptible to manipulation and subsequently elect a tyrant. The next 230 years has proven that we the public do **not** need to be held "in-check" for electing someone with whom we trust and has our best interest at heart. What has been proven is the Electoral College system is flawed in that three times a President has been elected against the will of the popular vote. I dare ask, did this system save us from electing a tyrant or is this just simply a byproduct flaw of

119

the system? I declare that we as individuals assume a direct vote responsibility with the wisdom, confidence, and trust for each other that we already possess.

Technology has revolutionized our lives. It has connected us like never before; we can now share and distribute information, ideas, data, and images almost instantly. What is being proposed here is a revision to our political system that allows each of us to participate in a part of the legislative branch of government on issues that affect you.

We will use a technology based government that allows the people to be active participants in government decisions. The systemic change allows American citizen to have a real voice and play an active role in the way we build and shape our communities. We the people have political clout, and it is time we use it. Let us make our vote count and not get muddled in the science of politics that moves district lines or uses obscure electoral voting techniques as the system of party elections.

It is absolutely amazing to draw a parallel from the might of the Roman Empire, whose network of roads with the chariot messengers gave them an ability to communicate and a distinct advantage over countries that challenged their supremacy. Now our entire world has a communication system that works without any delays. This communication system does not alleviate the need for effective leadership, but it opens the door to unprecedented means of a democratic government. Serving the citizens of a community should not involve power and corporate cash to influence the way one serves.

The ability we have with our communication system to disseminate information instantly, and even tally the public response in real time, has made it possible for We the People to be the voice in the House of Representatives. If we think about the technology used on election night, doesn't it make sense to use this level of communication to where we could have a participate in our government, try to put an end to bipartisan bickering, and let the democratic system of majority work for us?

House of Representatives

Harnessing the creativity of our citizen's ideas and voices means to be heard, considered and appropriately added on. This modification combined with an altered economic system will help us come to the realization that we have no limits to what can be accomplished in the way of services that are created for mankind by mankind.

Our current federal government system looks like this:

Figure 4.1

At the time the House of Representatives was created, it made sense because there was not a communication system or the means of transportation for common people to play an active role. So the House of Representatives was created so the people of the area they served would have an active voice in government. The question is: Do you believe that your District Representatives speaks for you? Do you even know who he/she is, let alone what they are trying to accomplish on your behalf?

With one amendment to our Constitution, the technology that connects us today would make it now possible for We the People to have an active voice in our government. And not just at the Federal level. We can choose to be more active at the community level as well.

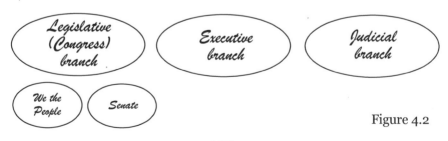

Figure 4.2

In the current system, the House of Representatives speaks for their constituents and simply represents half of the Legislative branch of our government. If we look to this solution, we must recognize the need for leadership. We must recognize the need for representation and a hierarchy of resources: the Senate, the President, Mayors, Governors, Principles, Superintendents of Schools, and all layers of leadership are necessary. When "we the people" become active as the House of Representatives, we will find born leaders among us.

This is not a proposal of anarchy; it is simply using the communication abilities that we have in a way that allows the "by the people" to actually be involved in their government. This government system will give individuals a voice and bridle the creative ideas of our citizens to help create beautiful communities. The President, our Governors, Mayors, etc. will remain the leaders of our government agencies. Our country will continue to work with much of the same structure and branches of government we have come to know. The people will empower the President to lead our country — let us not forget we need leadership to unite us. We must have vision to direct our future, to provide a moral compass, and help give us purpose.

Will 100% of people exercise their right to vote every time? No. But currently in non-presidential years between 30-40% of us cast our vote (the lowest of any democratic country), and when we are deciding on the President, about half of us mail in our votes or turn out to vote. We want to improve on the apathy we as a whole have, and we can only do that if we honestly feel like we have a voice in our government that works for us as its citizens. By having a voice we can reinstall confidence in our government.

As we are directly involved in our own House of Representation, and given our expansive resource of the economic system proposed here, we would also look at an expansive role of the Senate. This role would give them more available resources from the people they serve. Imagine the possibilities with the role of our leaders being shifted from deciding where to cut budgets to using their leadership skills to bring people together in creating and developing what we know is possible. This would enable them to respond to the creative ideas and needs of the people so that government not only helps drafts legislation for a community vote, but also so that we can coordinate, pool, and share resources necessary for projects that utilize the abilities of our citizens and best serve our country and our communities.

Using our communication technology in this political system, the people will have a chance to post ideas to share. If these ideas gain enough support, the champions of that bill work with the Senate to review possibilities, concerns, and draft legislation for a vote. Through these efforts, the government can help coordinate project support, the flow of material, prepare teams, manning and providing for the general welfare, progress, and even our defense. If used properly, we can pool resources; ensure communication, and oversee projects proposed by people or groups within our municipalities.

There are too many of us with great ideas and far too many of us that are not only willing but wanting to help the greater good of mankind. It is our government and economic systems that restrict us. With plenty of resources and continued technological advancements all around us, if we are afforded the chance to use them wisely, they could make for an amazing world where we can respond to the environmental needs of our planet and the growing needs of our community. This is the way for us to take full advantage of our advancements and abundant resources while simultaneously harnessing the incredible power of altruism instilled in human beings.

A People Involved Government

On the following page is a chart representing the flow of how our ideas would be made into a project or law.

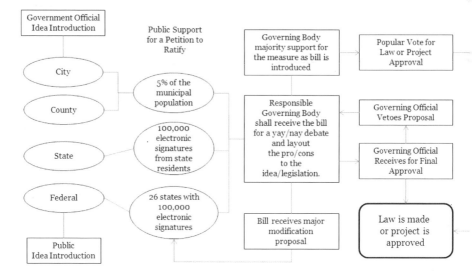

Figure

With people involved in government through the use of social technology, any person can submit an idea for a law or a project, even if it is just a stop sign or a park. If an idea gains enough support then it is submitted to the governing body for review and debate. If this bill stays as it was presented then the governing body agreesm and it is submitted back to the people's vote as it falls within that sphere of influence. Next it goes to the Mayor, Governor, or even the President for final ratification.

However, if the governing body propose changes to bill, this is routed back for a show of public support, and then it is once again routed through the approval or veto process.

If, after a show of public support, the governing body has also shown support and the leader of such an agency still vetoes the idea, the bill can be returned for public endorsement. The bill with the leader's argument shall go back to the people for a 2/3 endorsement, and if the governing body also endorses the bill, it shall then be approved.

Real change and unlimited potential in the power of the people will only come about if two things are changed, (1) the system of government in which we rule ourselves and (2) the economic system in which we regulate what can and cannot be done.

Our Economy

"Everybody can be great...because everybody can serve. You don't have to have a college degree to serve. You don't have to make your subject and verb agree to serve. You only need a heart full of grace. A soul generated by love."

Dr. Martin Luther King Jr.

The change that we desire, the change that we hope and ask for with each election is tied to our economic system. The difficult task for us as a public is to realize that it is not too big to change. That there is a way for us as citizens of the United States to truly be a leader of the free world.

From a positive perspective, it could be viewed that our current economic system has fostered a sense of greed that may have played a vital role in the advancement and discoveries within our society. I believe that we as a people want to believe that there is a direct parallel of people wanting to become rich and doing something good in the serving of mankind. But the question begs to be asked: is it the monetary reward that truly drives most people to create a service or product that may benefit mankind? Was Thomas Edison or Henry Ford truly driven by the thought that they would have great material riches? It is interesting that studies prove money in the workplace is definitely not the leading factor of satisfaction; it is appreciation. Think for a second how you feel when you do anything and it is simply not appreciated.

However, the greatest burden to our world society is that of our economic system. It restricts our ability to contribute and enjoy the abundance that this earth provides. In addition, it is the dollar that classifies man, not necessarily the content of his character. The notion of change immediately evokes thoughts of far-fetched; impossibility, improbability, that a similar concept has been tried, or possibly the idea is simply too large for most of us to wrap our heads around. Please let me assure you that a detailed plan and vision has not been seen by the American people in well over 200 years. We **are** the generation that can fix the problem associated with our current economic system and right the distrust we currently have for our current government.

In truth, the changes we make to vital programs and efforts to overhaul systems like healthcare or the tax code do little to truly affect us as citizens. They still exist under the umbrella of an existing economic system that is the root of a laundry list of problems that are growing rapidly in nature.

We have reached a level of satiety where we all feel that we have enough in the way of creating efficiencies within our production systems, and now we may see them working against us and have actually become fearful of our advancements. With our technological advancement and a competitive world economy, I would content that what we have created is instability in our ability to provide for our family. Our world economic system has simply become too volatile. How does it feel to hear that someone has been replaced by a machine or their jobs shipped overseas?

According to the US Census' international data, 60% of the world's population lives below the poverty line. When you combine the amount of poverty that exists on our planet and the simple hardship that we as average citizens endure while making ends meet, it becomes clear that it is our economic system that puts stress on our families. It is our monetary system that has become a huge burden, and now this system lies on the brink of collapse.

According to the World Food Program run by the United Nations, hunger kills more than all of the leading diseases combined (aids, malaria, and tuberculosis). The World Food Program (www.wfp.org)

illustrates the world poverty issue through the simple fact that 925 million people do not have enough to eat. That is more people going hungry than total populace of the United States, Canada, and the European Union combined.

According to the www.worldhunger.org, the world produces enough food to feed everyone. World agriculture produces 17% more calories per person than it did 30 years ago, even though there has been a 70% population increase. The principal problem is that many people in the world do not have sufficient land/conditions to grow or produce food or the income to purchase enough food. As of late November 2011, the world's population eclipsed 7 billion mark, and one in every seven of us spends the day hungry. This is a result of an economic system that is unable to sustain an entire population. There is a great chasm that continues to widen as the rich getting richer and poor getting poorer.

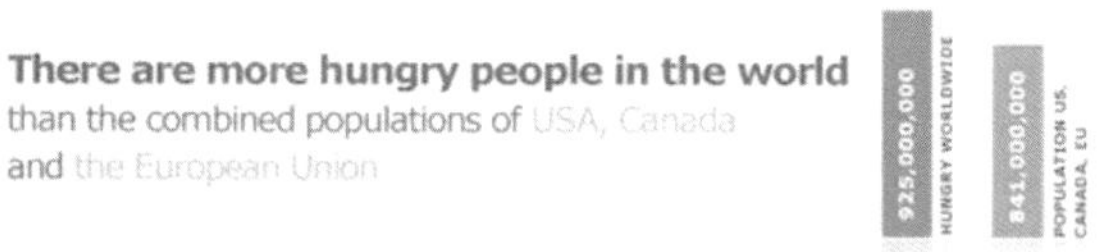

There are more hungry people in the world than the combined populations of USA, Canada and the European Union

925,000,000 HUNGRY WORLDWIDE

841,000,000 POPULATION US, CANADA, EU

Figure 4.4

Listening to micro-economic predictions is somewhat like listening to the experts predict the outcome of the World Series – it is all theory, our entire monetary system is based on theory. The short of it is that our economic system faces a complete collapse. We have begun to see glimpses with bank bailouts so ATM cards will continue to work, wrestling the question of whether we can continue to take care of our senior population with social security and Medicare. European countries are on the brink of collapse, and the United States is facing a financial cliff. We have already seen this kind of collapse in Iceland, once touted as a thriving capitalistic society, and now a failed country forced to take on a socialist government and economic system. The list of failing economies continues to grow with Greece, Spain and Portugal facing real hardships.

When Obama first took office, the United States debt was at $9 trillion, 22 cents out of every dollar went to pay that interest. As our debt sails past $16 trillion ($46,000 for every man woman and child) at a rate of about $6 million/minute, the interest cost that strains our tax dollars mean that more cuts are imminent as our economic system heads towards a series of fiscal cliffs. As our previous head of accounting stated and our current country's comptroller agreed, our current path of economics is unsustainable. You can't really argue against those assertions. As we head towards a government that can barely afford much more than its own interest payments, and eventually towards a complete financial meltdown, as the US dollar is the standard and the engine of the world economy our economic woes will have a global affect.

People that protest about the disparity of our economic system, who rant and rave about the separating of the 1% and general population of the 99% that simply try to pay the bills remain stifled at the thought that it's possible for a true change to come with our existing monetary system. The notion of change to this system may seem overwhelming or even impossible, but it begins with a trust and belief that as a nation united, we as a people can do anything — even recreate our world.

There is a fundamental shift in our economic system that is being proposed and detailed here. Instead of budgets dictating whether a good or service can be provided, it is simply up to the will of the provider and it is our gratitude for each other's contribution that fuels our desire to give more to each other – this is the natural law of altruism. It is the need of community that fuels the vacuums of required contributors.

Contribution Card System

The change proposed for the economic system is tied to the principles of altruism or tapping the desire of individuals to help others and in study of human nature of what drives us to help even more is that of knowing that what we give will be returned. This Contribution Card System gives us that assurance every time we ask of someone to provide a good or service. Additionally, this fills the gap by providing the appreciation for each other we currently lack in our established economic system.

In a society where we are free to serve, you need to be ready to answer the question that we hear a lot today: "What do you do?" It is the appreciation we have for each other's contribution that we use as currency. A system based on trust, a system in which we care for each other, our needs are met, and we live in abundance.

> *""Life's most persistent and urgent question is: 'What are you doing for others?*

> **Dr. Martin Luther King Jr.**

Take a moment to think about your willingness to participate in a greater cause. Are you willing to work to make our country great and enrich your community by giving what you believe others will appreciate? Think about the stories where our country pulled together, sacrificed, and contributed resources for the efforts of World War II, or how we felt the unity of coming together as Americans shortly after the terror attacks on 9/11/01. We are all the same willing people, and the truth is we don't need to be in a war to be motivated; we simply need to have purpose. When we are given purpose and a clear vision of a societal restructure more aligned with our innate desires, the only question is, "What are you willing to do to help others"?

Under this Contribution System, before you can ask of goods or services you must be prepared to share your card with those you are asking so that they can see what you have done for others. In addition the person receiving that which you have given must be willing to provide feedback to that person or organizations that have provided a good or a service.

When you contribute or work as part of a company or organization, your contribution efforts is recorded using technology like that of a credit card. When you receive goods or services your receipt is your expression of appreciation or dissatisfaction. We use this record of contribution and appreciation when asking others for goods and services we desire. Not as a currency in the sense of debits and credits, but in the spirit of altruism where we know that we give of ourselves and it is indeed reciprocated and given back to us. For those with bad records then it up to us as industry servers to decide whether or not we serve them.

It is this method that we use to build trust, to build community, and foster an even deeper sense of desire to give more in an altruistic way. The basic system would look like:

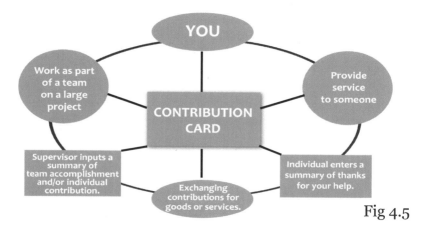

Fig 4.5

With a *Contribution Card* – each card provides an open book *accounting system of appreciation* for each other's work acknowledged with gratitude from the recipient much in the simple method eBay uses as feedback of its seller's (example fig 4.6). This is the mechanism by which we recognize each other's altruistic gifts that we give; this is the means by which we realize that if I scratch your back, you are indeed scratching mine. This along with the leadership and a system of identifying needs will be enough for us all to live in abundance.

Fig 4.6

Contribution Card Report

Name: _Jeff Vileta_   Date: **12/25/20xx**

Date	Contribution Summary	Contribution Type
12 years	Compucom Corporation - helps people find work	Ongoing company
12/24/12	Blanket drive - made and passed out 500 blankets to the Childrens Hospital for incoming patients	Community
12/20/12	Church choir - sang for the holiday season	Community
11/25/12	PTA - helped with school homecoming dance	Education

Appreciation

Date	Message	From
12/20/12 -	Thank you so much for connecting me with the Microsoft opportunity. it was just the career position I was looking for.	Jen Olson Database Programmer
12/18/12 -	We are so excited about our new release of Club Penguin and could not have done it without your help. Thank you so much for helping us find the web development talent we needed.	Disney Online (company)

Fig 4.7

Of course there are details that need to be worked through, and of course we will need to work with system architects to create the infrastructure, systems, and hardware necessary to transition to such a system, but none of what we are talking about has not already been in-place in some sort of fashion. Our entire financial system is already digitally, stored on computers with transactions recorded with the swipe of a magnetic strip. It is our technological advances that have made this possible. It is our advances that, if harnessed correctly, can create a beautiful means of caring for ourselves that translates into the ability to create a much stronger family unit, thus community. This could forever close the gap of the haves and the have-nots.

Similar to many other data systems, The Contribution Card as a common exchange of information has some other values. Streamlining our information system can clear the waters of immigration and lines at the post office, DMV and other government agencies that seem to be operate with everyone waiting with the Well Connected People we have a system of information that let us embrace our efficiencies with every agency or company that serves.

Industry meetings are a place for people to get together and enjoy each other's company, talk strategy, share jobs, look for help, and in general talk shop as collaborators. Within our new economic structure, these talks can be of collaboration meant to help build community rather than competing to provide a desired product or service. A lot of the choices with regards to which industry you choose is because of the company you will keep, the kind of person you are, and the kind of person you best identify with. Because each team, each business, and each industry becomes a part of the success of our communities, our personal success depends on our success as a community. Naturally, being a part of something successful makes communities successful, and if communities are successful that means it's citizens are as well. Think about a community report given under these circumstances and all the good news that would come from it. Now compare that withthe news of today and the choices we are forced to make concerning what needs to be cut to make the budgets balance.

With the contributions of all who want to participate and contribute, there is a place that we can get to where there is no end and no restrictions to what can be accomplished. When it comes to a company hiring it is very similar to when we were kids on the playground, and someone came up to say, "I want to play," we had the option to either say "yes" or "no." This is similar to how it is now if you want to hire someone, only we will not be restricted by budgets, only needs of growth or an expanding scope of services. By expanding an organization's service, it makes the organization better.

There are concerns. Some worry about how real estate might work in our new economic system. Some worry about people taking advantage of automobiles available to them or how some may participate in excessive travel in such a system. The first thing that comes to mind is how it works at an all you can eat buffet:, no one can really eats more than their share but we can all work on our efficiency mentality. The fact is that industries that serve must be the regulator; they that wish to be a part of the real estate, automobile, leisure or travel industries must be a community upon themselves and work through ways they serve. With only a limit on what can be given, you can either serve all that want and have left overs or design the system in which there are restrictions. Similar to a church today that chooses to serve, they decide how and who they provide services to. Individuals, companies, and industries will be the ones that decide if they cannot serve 100% of the marketplace, how they will serve, and who they can. I envision basic rights to have a home, heat, food, water, and medical care. I envision timeshares being more prevalent for vacation houses, community boats or airplanes, much more sharing of resources with a higher level of trust leads to people working together becomes much more prevalent.

Let's take this opportunity to look at a few examples that might explain how some industries and services could work in this new economic system:

Say your organization provides a bull dozer service; maybe there are so many people that want to operate a bull dozer that the union that oversees the industry sets the expectations of what one must learn or what one must do to pay his/her dues to gain enough seniority to become a "certified" bull dozer operator. Similarly the real estate industry oversees their industry. Each industry and each factory or service organization must work together to establish their own rules and guidelines for the way they are able to serve the marketplace and the way those that desire to become part of that industry grow within it. Rules, laws, and guidelines must fit within this new found freedom.

Pause for a minute and think about how a transaction might look with a Contribution Card system. Let's use my Grandmother and the purchase of her new car as an example. She has had her eye on a red

Chevy Cavalier and has had her Oldsmobile for 10 years. So she goes to the car lot to talk with salesman. This used car salesman may have once been thought of as "sleazy" and approached with apprehension because of some sales/pressure tactics the industry may use today in "helping" us make a buying decision. Under the contribution system, we are all viewed as someone who helps each other, and now this sales person is in a position to say, "I have a car for you." He can give her his honest feedback and be an adviser on different options that may be best suited for her. Again you can only get a car by someone who works in this industry serving you. There must be standards, yes – 1 car/adult in your family – while yes this may be the goal of the industry. Might we give someone a collector status, sure that might be something for the industry server to decide. No longer does the dollar decide that which is served, no longer are we serving the dollar.

Within the structure of this system there grows trust and appreciation that fosters a relationship between the giver and the person desiring goods or services. Given that he is in the automobile business and the supply is right, he may have the connection to get that Cavalier for Grandma and the knowledge of the automobile so that she can drive away with confidence. He looks at her Contribution Card and sees some of the glowing reviews from people she has made rugs for and other related sewing jobs that she has taken on. In reality, it may be that she has served a lot of her family, some friends, some neighbors, and a few couples she met over the internet whom were getting married. However, it is our ability to serve our community within our own sphere of influence that could easily be enough. In addition, she helped make sandwiches for people who helped pick the tomato crop this last summer. She serves within her sphere of influence and helps where she can, and for those she has helped, you can see how much she is appreciated by the write ups of thanks credited to her card. All the salesman needs to see is that she has been willing to help others, and he is now in a position to help her. This transaction fosters gratitude for each other. The salesman himself may have a daughter that is getting married and could use some of her sewing expertise. All of these transactions help foster community. As we learn more about what we do for each other, we open the door to new relationships. Given that he is in the automobile industry, he can look at her automobile history to ensure she is not abusing the system and doesn't have a collection of idle automobiles in a shed somewhere. He can see that she has driven a 1998 white Oldsmobile for 10 years, and he agrees he can help her into the newer car she is looking for.

Here is another scenario. Let's take a look at how the Real Estate market might work and the role of the real estate agent. Under the current system a real estate agent must try and find customers. They need to network, pass out business cards, send out marketing mailing, cold call, or wait countless hours at an open house in hopes of finding a willing client. It would be hard to argue that if a real estate agent does a good job today they are not very much appreciated. How can you not be thankful for someone who found you the home you are looking for and helped put the pieces together to make it work? Under the Contribution Card system, we would have to look to the real estate industry to develop their own rules and guidelines for which people are selected on the home they wish to own. Under this new system, we must rely on the industries that serve to provide the guidelines for which they can serve with what they have. Ideally, when a family is in need of a new home, the agent will first understand their situation and they would use their knowledge of market and neighborhoods to make good fits to help build strong neighborhoods and good communities. Their knowledge of neighborhoods would serve communities in harmony with all of the goods and services we provide each other. Second, third, and multiple homes would give way to timeshare vacation homes where people share in the responsibilities.

In this system, the pressure is removed in the worry of making a sales and commission. The pressure of commission is removed, and the despair of a day waiting for someone to come in to hear our sales pitch is over. As the circle of the system continues to churn, so does our innate desire to help each other. I It is our recognition and appreciation for one another's contribution that inspires us to give and give even more from an altruistic heart. We must remember that appreciation is a much greater motivator than that of the dollar.

We are far more willing to give and it much easier for us as people **to** give than it is to receive. When volunteering for my daughter's school I had organized a clothes swap. The concept was simple: bring the clothes you would like to get rid of and if you found something you liked or needed, please feel free to take whatever you needed. There were some that approached it with fear and thought we needed to put limits on what was taken. But my response was, "If you could use it, take it." I believe in the good of people, and as such there were no restrictions. This was/is a school that offers a high percentage of reduced lunches. However, at the end of the event, we had many bags of good clothes left over to give to other causes. It is very interesting how we are made as people, and that it is far easier for us to give, especially when we experience the joy of the receiver and sometimes how difficult it is to receive.

Do you think we might approach each other differently? Like the used car salesman, I really just want to feel like I am helping others. What we all want are the means to support ourselves and our family and enjoy the gifts that life has to offer.

Can you see how these transactions do not carry any stigma of fear and how we can grow to appreciate each other? We no longer fear that we can't afford something. We simply in good conscience believe we deserve a good or service for which we ask. This is made easier when we feel good about our own contributions. By our asking, we foster our own desire to give. These are the natural laws of altruism. We no longer fear that the sales person is going to try to take advantage or try to sell us a bunch of masked problems. In this new system, we can appreciate each other and are likely to recommend each other's service to friends and family. Everything lends to fostering and growing connections within our community.

What happens if we find someone who does not have a medical reason for not working? Or what if it appears they have simply been laying on their couch not fulfilling commitments or making any effort to contribute using one of the multitude of opportunities available to them? A minimum system could be instilled on things like groceries. That would be a decision for the grocery/food industry – but let us consider how much we throw away. It would be a decision for all of us whether we would want to provide a good or service to anyone or simply make a recommendation of what you see in the way of opportunities for someone to make an effort to be a productive member of society. This would be very similar to my daughter's elementary school. When they run out of lunch money on their ticket, the kids are forced to receive the minimal peanut butter sandwich and that is motivation enough to get back to their parents for lunch alternatives. Each industry and each individual serving that sector, whether it food, real estate, auto, etc., will come up with their own guidelines, their own minimums, and their own maximums for serving the community.

We receive the most satisfaction by helping people and being appreciated. Within our current system and our current economic environment, there is too much pressure to sell that car to survive. Because of that, most of the true enjoyment about being a car salesman has been removed. Car salespersons don't want to think of their customers as suckers, and we don't want to work with anyone that we think is sleazy. They, like all of us, simply want to help and be appreciated as a valued part of the community. Furthermore, all of our time is of value. All sales professional under this contribution system could work by appointments rather than waiting countless hours for the next "up" to walk on the lot.

Our new economic system puts the responsibility of those who provide services or products squarely on those who create or give those services. We as the giver now have complete control. It's the givers who determine who gets and who does not. Remember those who help with the goods and services that we desire, they do so because they choose to and their first thoughts are to serve not exclude. Teams band together as a company working with other companies cohesively. The goal is to serve as many people as possible or to fully provide their chosen place in the marketplace with great abundance. The truth is, when the industry is served fully, then we have the timeto go home, be with our family, look for other means of serving, practice in our creative outlets, or learn. I can only imagine the pride that comes from being part of an industry that fully serves.

Economy Summary

By participating in solutions rather than competing against each other, not only will we be promoting communities filled with harmony, but we as citizens will be welcomed contributors and participants in our government instead of passive observers of the news we see on networks like CNN or Fox News. Our country is at a critical time, where we can either do something that unites us or we can we can become victims to the collapse and be left to wonder what will happen in the power vacuum.

Economic theory 101 is that we are at maximum GNP right now, and the only way to increase one item of our market is to decrease another. So we use money to keep the demand in balance. Our economic system and its <u>theories</u> raise many questions. What happens when the supply of money is reduced due to the continual supply of unsustainable deficit spending? I'll tell you: budget cuts reduce the demand of goods and services, but these good and services are still available. With government spending, we can have an effect on our economy. Conversely, when that spending dries up we can see our government become a huge burden and strain to our economic system.

Does a reduced money supply suddenly decrease the amount of raw goods available to produce the goods we use or somehow reduce the willingness of our citizens to provide services we have come to appreciate? Or does this work in reverse? The reduced supply of money restricts the ability of people who want to provide goods and services. So many things about our system leave us all shaking our heads and thinking that is simply not right.

The practice of market prediction, whether it will fluctuate up or down, and no one really knowing for certain seems like a ridiculous system for a society. As does a private institution profiting from our country's debt, and a whole list of society hypocrisies. While gambling remains illegal in many parts, our entire economic system operates as one big casino with $10 trillion being moved simply as a daily bet on the best return.

We have come to a place where we serve money more than we serve each other producing tangible goods and providing meaningful services to each other. What is being proposed here is a chance to write a new contract with America. Let's put it on the ballot for the American people to vote on a change to the economic system. Let's embrace our efficiencies and have this truly translate into more equality, more quality time with our family, and more promoting and building connection and acceptance within community.

The system being proposed is designed to allow us the luxury of giving more to our communities, provide an acceptance for anyone to make a meaningful contribution, and to promote individual creativity. We are talking about an economic system that uses technology to track our contributions as a "good will" currency if you will. A system based on altruism that we give because it is in our heart to give and we know that it is what is needed for the greater good. We give because it is within us to give, and we can honestly live a life looking for ways to help people while knowing our own needs are met. The great gift we receive in return is that of being appreciated, and a society that frees us to spend more time to develop the relationships with the one's we care about most – making for a much strong family unit.

Acceptance of the Contribution Economic system means that we disburden ourselves with budgets. We do however burden ourselves with finding the resources and the manpower necessary to accomplish what needs to be accomplished. What this means is that there are opportunities to help and get involved all around us – full employment would exist, and there would always be an opportunity to pitch in.

We are now put into a position of appreciation. We now are all in a position to be grateful for those who want to help us. Whether it is finding a new car; moving into a house; obtaining steel for some manufacturing idea you may have; medical treatments; painting; concerts; and just about everything we have come to appreciate as a society in the way of goods and services, shifting our focus of serving money to serving people and making contributions for the greater good is the key to building a community that welcomes and appreciates you as a part of it.

Summary

We all know that something needs to be done, that we may be facing an economic collapse, and that we have a government that we simply do not trust. We want something to be done, and unless we do the hard work, we the people will probably never see the changes we want.

"Human progress never rolls in on the wheels of inevitability; it comes through the tireless efforts of people willing to be co-workers with God."

Dr. Martin Luther King Jr.

We all want to do something, but we have to find out what that something is if we want true reform. As President Clinton put it, "It is always much easier to do what you did yesterday." Understand that change and transition is painful. Understand that a change of this magnitude leads us down a path we have never been. But if we approach this change together, we can find comfort in knowing that we are united, we can do this together as a unified country filled with hope and promise. Yes! There are unknowns. Yes! There is work to be done. But yes! we can take comfort in knowing we can trust and rely on each other.

We recognize that there are concerns that others may try to take advantage of the system and try to get by while doing nothing. But we need to remember two things. First, we aren't a perfect system without corruption. I Is it right that a trust baby really should have to contribute? Two, we need to recognize that these people are held accountable to you and me. If someone comes to you looking for a good/service that you provide and their contribution does not meet your standards, then you can suggest ways they can get involved and make a greater contribution. Let them then come back again to ask if they may have what you are providing.

This is a fundamental shift away from money as the dictator of power and no one really caring how this power or money is derived. This shift leads us to a system in which the provider chooses whether a product or service is provided. Our thinking of appreciation shifts from that of the money to that of provider, giving all of us thankful positions in jobs we're well-suited for. We will find an appreciation to all who give, thereby all of us experiencing being appreciated.

So we have seen the details of the three constitutional amendments that lay the path to a true systemic change for the political and economic systems of our United States of America. Detailed in Chapter 8 lies the method of change by which we utilize the system that is put in-place within our Constitution to make such a change. Let us recognize this plan as a frame work within which many industries will face new challenges and decisions to be made. In that same breadth, let us also recognize that these industries won't be facing decisions on survival. Instead, they will be creating methods to serve in the spirit of collaboration with other companies rather than cutthroat competition. In the spirit of serving, everyone benefits. In the spirit of love and giving, all things are possible. In the spirit of fear and doubts of others, we restrict ourselves and hinder personal and communal growth.

Does this plan put in-place an answer for every industry, the judicial system, limits or methods of collaboration? Did Henry Ford have the plan for fuel distribution, roadways, how to make stop lights, maintenance plans, or an eventual freeway system? No, we must be confident and trust that if we provide a new framework and understand that benefits and possibilities, we as a people can help make it work.

It has been documented and stated that the forefathers and authors of our Constitution outlined a structure for our government to be By the People for the People not of the corporation for the interest of the corporation. It is time we take back our government, put the trust in ourselves, and provide more resources to the agencies and companies that serve us. Let's put a stop to all of these unnecessary cuts and trying to do more with less mentality. Abundance is all around us: there is plenty of food to feed the world, there are plenty of people willing to work, everything we need has been provided. It is simply up to us to create the systems in which we live that will best utilize our resources, not restrict our desires and abilities to serve, and allow us all to enjoy the abundance that should be available to us.

Our current system restricts our ability to help because of what we must serve first - the dollar! Think for a second how much time is spent serving the dollar versus simply creating or serving another? Of its huge markets, the financial and insurance industries all serve the dollar and not mankind. And not only does the budget of the dollar restrict our ability to help, but it makes it much more difficult than it has to be. It generates a huge amount of waste in trying to account for the value of our services and how our dollar should be taxed and reported. The bottom line is that our economic system both restricts us and is providing a burden that we as a society will not be able to bear much longer.

This restriction of our current economic system limits our abilities to build new roads, pay more teachers, or simply afford appropriate housing. It has created a growing chasm between the 1% of the wealthy and the 99%, which we say are the have-nots. Instead of living in abundance, we struggle to pay our bills on a monthly basis.

Within this Contribution system proposed here, the entire "accounting" system is automated, and the "checks and balances" occur every time we provide or ask for a transaction. Should there be "watch dogs" within this proposed system? Yes, we should be ready to help people whenever and wherever they need it. That is how we are made. We desire to help people. We take joy in helping others, and that includes helping others become healthy both physically and mentally and become productive members of our society.

Under this proposed Contribution Card system, we leverage the advances made in technology. Technological advancements have helped connect us like never before. Technology has given us the conduit to move a lot of information in split-second time. But this new technology has made our workforce part of the $10 trillion dollar daily world casino where money and jobs are moved around the world trying to make the best return for the owners. Stability is a rare commodity in today's workforce. However, if this new information age is harnessed properly, it can help in the growth of our connections to family and community.

There are so many pioneers in this country that have been given a lot of credit for creating so many things: the light bulb, the telephone, automobiles. Still, the pioneers and innovators of the computer age have reshaped our world and our communication abilities forever. In a decade, we have exploited our technology capabilities in amazingly good ways. Letters gave way to faxes, faxes to emails, land lines to cell phones... we are all connected like never before if we chose to be, and information exchanges hands while we are talking. We need to use this not to create a greater means of competing globally to provide goods and services, but instead we much use technology as a means of us all growing in our contribution to mankind. The right to appreciate and be appreciated will put a whole new face on all of our contributions and the way we face work. However you decided to help, if someone needs your product or service, then we are no longer under the oppression of the golden rule, "Those who have the gold make the rules." That kind of rule fosters arrogance and subservient classes of people instead of fostering an appreciation for one another. If you are cared for with food, shelter, medical treatment, and even entertainment, don't you think you will be in a position to not only want to contribute but also appreciate others contribution? And if you are unburdened by having to serve money first, don't you feel that you will look for ways to join in the service of your community? Could you not believe that not having to worry about finding a job but knowing there are opportunities everywhere would be a good thing?

Removing the work week from huge markets (like the financial and insurance sectors) opens up the opportunity to work on creative expression and spend more time with those we appreciate the most. Positions of appreciation is what our current society lacks. Too many people out there are working and feeling like not only a number, but a disposable number at that. People are not appreciated for the contribution that they are making, and therefore they are disconnected from their company because of the disposable employee climate in which we live and the sub-servant way we view each other. The thought that firing, layoffs, and cutbacks are not only common place but simply accepted as part of our system – all are a lot of things, but good is not one of them. For a societal restructuring to work, the most important factor is that we start by deciding for ourselves. Too many elections are tilted in one direction or another because people's votes are made in consideration of what other people will do. In this vote for an Amended Constitution, you must decide for yourself. You must not cast a vote because you have concern for what someone else will do. This time it is about you. We need to pause and remember how similar we really are and let our own conscience be heard through our vote. These are the seeds of real change. Find strength in your own conviction for what you feel is right.

The system of voting works, and when used properly it glorifies our democracy and what we all agree as Americans is the best way to govern. This proposal is about giving the voter back their voices and allowing us to truly elect a governing body of our choosing. Let's be a government that is truly "By the People, For the People".

United by a plan of clarity, we can create a system that turns complaints into constructive ideas that we can all evaluate as ideas for the betterment of our community. This proposal asks of us as communities to play a much more active role in that of serving ourselves within our government. It also provides for an economic structure where you are needed and creative participation is welcomed. United, we can be on the path to making a change away from being on the cusp of another budget cut; or the casualty of a job that has been outsourced; or our country falling off a series of fiscal cliffs.

These changes root out the corruption in our government caused by special and self-interests. These systemic changes focus our energies in serving the greater good.

It is far too easy to blame someone else for the transgressions of the country or the world and passively say that "they" should do something about it. I have heard enough people saying, "I have an idea.". It is time "we" become the "they" and play an active role in creating our better nation. I It starts with petitioning. This is about banding together, becoming active participants, and giving everyone a voice and the means to make changes that make sense. To stop the finger pointing at the "they" for the problems and start counting on the "we" to make a real difference. Together with a shared vision, we make it possible. Fortunately, this great land of ours has been shaped by some of the finest, most giving, hardest working, stressed out bunch of American working stiffs. And we as Americans have a right to be proud of who we are. We are creative, smart, resourceful and determined. It is humorous and somewhat enlightening to remember that most of our ancestors who came to this country were misfits and rejects willing to chance everything on an unknown and a dream of something better. We have seen our country unite as brothers and sisters after the tragedies of 9/11; we have sacrificed through World

Wars; we all do our part to conserve when water or other resources become scarce. Harnessing this power of community and purpose opens the door to amazing possibilities. Building stronger families and beautiful communities while fostering a system of trust. That is what these changes are about ladies and gentleman. We can replace the fears that we live with. Additionally, when we first change things within our country's boundaries, and we will be in a better position to help the entire world. Together we can change everything and truly make the world a better place. It may be ambitious, but this could even lead to the means of world peace.

If we really want to open our eyes, we will see that the real reason that our monetary system faces failure is not because of incorrectly managing balance sheets, a lack of growth, or even our citizens working hard enough. At the root, it is simply that our system is based on fear. We are held down by the simple fear that we cannot find someone willing to trade our pelt of fur for a pair of shoes, the fear that we cannot find someone to barter with for the things we need. We grew up with this fear that we don't have any alternative to money.

We may find that the system requires some sort of minimum hourly contribution. We may find that we need some sort of minimum GNP standard. We may find ourselves without tomatoes if no one is willing to help harvest the crop. However, if we as individuals are counted on as appreciated and welcomed members of a team, then we as a people will respond in kind. Let us embrace a system that aids in the exchange of goods and services. Let us embrace a system that drastically reduces waste. Let us embrace the possibilities of a system that speaks to and promotes an inherent good that lies within all of us. Let us let go of a system that fosters lying, cheating, stealing, corruption, greed, and suspicion at every level. Let us recognize that it is the system and circumstances from which we live that shape our reactions. This inherit good was found in Iraq; there was far less fighting when the people had meaningful work and the means to care for their families. This system gives everyone that opportunity to have meaningful work and feel the appreciation of their contribution.

The ABC show Extreme Makeover is a perfect example of how we as citizens are willing to give of ourselves and come together for the people of a community. In this television show, families with special needs are identified who are suffering in inadequate housing because they cannot afford anything different. The organizers tell their story, and the community rallies to help tear down their existing home that does not meet their needs. The community pitches in to help build one that better fits their needs. The house is rebuilt in record time, the family returns, and you can see the payoff in the appreciation pouring out of the recipients family's eyes. The community comes together, joining in the efforts and the celebration of having given something wonderful to one of their members that truly had prayers answered. Looking into the eyes of someone who is truly grateful for your efforts is always enough if our own needs are being met. It is our giving that makes us whole; it is so interesting how we are all hard wired this way. (And yes, of course you could find an example of some ornery son of a bitch that may be used an exception.)

The same holds true with the stories shared from the Habitat for Humanity efforts. When we focus on such efforts, we begin to realize truly how good we as a people really are and how willing we are to help. We as a people are much more willing to be a part of the body of work when we know we are needed. Being a part of such efforts has much more in the way of personal rewards compared to simply making a donation to the next worthy cause. This is especially true when faced with doubts about where the money is really going.

In our current society, being a successful business, having a medical practice, or working as a farmer, you need a good marketing and sales plan. To be successful in sales, you have to get out there and take rejection after rejection from uninterested folks until you find the one person who does. Even after that, your continued growth relies on referrals or successful marketing plans or sustained sales efforts. That's why we get so much junk mail: because we know that a marketing plan must canvas an area to find that possible 1% that may be interested.

Attached to the end of this book is a petition. With a million signatures per state, we call on each state to apply for an Article V Convention. We call on this convention to draft a bill to include the following three Constitutional Amendments:

1) Abolishment of the electoral college
2) Establishment of the well-connected people as the House of Representatives
3) Acceptance of the Contribution economic system

With clear and definitive language, the Constitution requires that this convention be held when 2/3 of the states apply for it.. If we the people make it clear why we are convening this Convention, then a bill is drafted for public vote. If we the people vote to pass this bill with a vote of greater than 75%, then the change we have been asking for with each election truly happens.

Chapter 5   Our Psyche, Our Soul

& How It Fits With Social Change

The prince and the peasant will not be equaled by cutting off the prince's head.

Mahatma K. Gandhi

INTRODUCTION

Change does not come about by war, rioting, or even a revolution. Change is deeply rooted in love. This chapter is about the mindset required to lead a systemic change to our economic system and a structural modification to our government. We're not after an obscure piece of legislation that makes such a small difference that we can't feel it. Our goal is something that without a doubt creates a real difference in every American's life the moment it goes into effect. Thoughts of revolution and changes in our personal lives conjure up excitement, fear, simple uncertainty, and a host of other emotions. This chapter looks at the psychology of social change, how our beliefs affect our ability to accept change, and love versus fear when dealing the struggle for justice and equality.

First, let us take comfort in the fact that there is a mechanism built into our Constitution that makes it possible for the people to influence changes through the amendment process. Furthermore, it was the intent and the hope of our forefathers that we would change the

161

structure of our society when it is needed – change is how it is supposed to be. This is possible through peaceful and non-violent means, promoting the message of altruism and using a petition as the instrument to show that we are united together in support of our state. It is time that we begin exercising our right to ask for a Constitutional Convention.

Let's begin by acknowledging the fact that no plan, no piece of legislation, and no great idea will be accepted by everyone. There is always someone that will not understand our position and has a reserved fear. Let us use education and our message to reach those that we can, and there will always be debate, there will always be a view shared from the "other side". Consensus is great but let us allow debate to expand our individual views.

But let us also be clear on one thing. We want individuals to decide for themselves to join the community that agrees without proposition. If we can grow as a community of like-minded people that believe in opening the door to acceptance and fullest potential as a society, then we can create a movement that grows and where everything becomes possible. However, all we can really do is share this message and this plan. For those who do not agree, we offer the following quote:

Reason is not automatic, those who deny it,
cannot be conquered by it, leave them alone.
Ayn Rand

We want to avoid any "us versus them" rhetoric that we might find so prevalent in our political culture today. So while we acknowledge the fact that not everyone may agree with our plan, let us open our arms for those that agree on the principles we hold dear, and let's welcome everyone's ideas and contributions during the execution of this protest. Let's band together to call for social change.

We will welcome everyone. We will welcome all creative ideas and input, and through collective reasoning our plan will grow and become better with the united people of the United States. We not only want to welcome everyone who wishes to participate, but we want ideas and talents that come from the value of diverse individual participation. When we understand the economic solution herein, we realize that we are debunking the myth that money regulates the demand in a theoretical effort to equalize it with supply. The truth is that global supply now grossly outweighs the demand according to Nobel economist Joseph Stiglitz. We have and create enough food to feed the world twice over, yet we throw away much of it, and we let 60% of the world go hungry because they cannot afford it.

It doesn't take a rocket scientist to realize that it's the budget restrictions that reduce our ability to purchase the products and services we may desire. It is also the budgets that restrict those who are working and force those, such as a single parent, to work multiple jobs to make ends meet. Furthermore, budgets and our current economic system restrict our seniors who may want to contribute but are forced to sit on the sidelines. It makes sense to review the fears that we may have. It is easy for someone to assume we may be talking about some form of anarchy, socialism, or even communism. That, however, is not what we are talking about here. What we are trying to instill is sense of regulated altruism in the way we offer each other goods and services. In a sense, we are looking to create a community of givers. These are givers of both of goods and services, and it is our goal to instill a sense of caring for one another.

The fear that we will have run away demand needs immediate debunking. We already have a taste of abundance in many areas of our lives, such the library where you could check out as many books as you like yet the shelves are still full. Our police and fire departments that are only a phone call away, yet we know that it is socially not acceptable to abuse the service. And like a community potluck where you can eat all you want, the truth is much is of it is wrapped up and returned. In addition, talking with the manager of sushi restaurant, satiety quickly reached her, and she was not interested in eating her own product anymore. The same happened with a Dairy Queen owner, while it may be considered some of the best ice cream, the very man who has unlimited access to it rarely touches it; he simply serves it to others. It amazes me that someone who has unfettered access to something quickly reaches the point of satiety and then simply takes joy in watching others enjoy.

The mindset of taking part in a revolution requires bravery. Perhaps it is not the kind of bravery required for taking up a sword and going to war, but a type of bravery with unfailing belief and a love for your fellow citizens. A type of bravery where our belief is that what we are doing is right and that when we accomplish what we set out to do, we will have created something more beautiful than we can presently imagine. We must begin by recognizing the similarities of man in the way we are created, that we all experience the same emotions, all have the same desires, and yet we all are different in our dreams of creating or our vision of giving.

As it applies to the system restructuring outlined here, you are not only being asked to participate, to support change, and vote that which is in your hearts. You are being asked to decide for yourself and vote your own conscience. We must agree that there is dignity in all work. Within each of our contributions come a dignity and a caring and giving community. Are you willing to help create a change our society to one that is filled with acceptance, love and appreciation? We shall let the democratic process work and hope we can educate and reach enough with this message. We must share the possibility and educate that there is a way to fix our government and our economic system.

This plan means we move from a society based on fear to one of love. That we move from a place of impossibility to a place of clarity, confidence, and possibility. Our United States Constitution not only outlines a method for change, but it also counted on continued bravery from its citizens. This bravery means that we must be willing to implement changes to the structure in order to fit the times. Our government and economic systems are in need of real change. Let us embrace the possibility, let us get involved and together we can truly change the minds of our society.

Our country and the world have undergone dramatic societal changes since our Constitution was introduced. These changes were unfathomable to the authors of our Constitution. Planes, automobiles, the assembly line, our communication system, and the ability to bake a potato in four minutes are just a handful of these changes. In addition, according to studies at Indiana University, each generation's IQ level increases, at least according to the data that has been captured over the past 60 years. At the root of all these changes still remains an overwhelming desire for people to simply be a welcomed part of community. Because how we are made as people in general have not changed.

Given our current times every successful politician must have a promising message of change. With every person's time in office, an unfulfilled promise, because the problems we face are larger than any one Senator, Governor, Mayor even President. As the fruit of the desire for change continues to ripen, we are frankly losing some of that audacity for hope. We are in the midst of a sea of citizens that but no one has really presented a plan that can transcend the colors of red or blue. Perhaps we have been waiting for a plan, perhaps it could be the one you are holding right here. Collectively we have begun to realize that a new piece of legislation or a newly elected candidate with "change" in their tagline is not enough. An amazing superstar legislator, a change to our healthcare system, our tax code, or our budget will never be enough to correct the problems we are having with the trust and confidence in our own government and that of our economy. We need real systemic change to our economic and government systems, if we are to experience that which we are truly asking for.

This chapter is meant to look at the fears that we have about a societal change and the common bond of our psychological makeup that flows through us all. It is also meant to look at our makeup as people and how we are hard wired and take these factors into consideration as framework for society. We also want take a closer look at the emotions of change and revolution. The intention of this chapter is to break open our psyche, to use the study of the human spirit, our tendencies to make sense of what makes us all so similar, and the traits we are born with. In doing so, we uncover the understanding of what unites us as common people and what makes us all part of the same fabric. It puts into the context our innate desires and the bondage of restrictions that we place on ourselves as a people that limit our ability for each of us to find self-actualization.

Every election has a candidate trying to bring the same message of hope and change. During a campaign, it is the candidate that can persuade us to believe that he or she can make the real changes to affect the love in our hearts, bring us together as family and community, and providing a better sense of security in the way we have provide for ourselves. Additionally, they strike at our sense of value in taking part in prosperity for all.

The reality is that the change we seek does not come about with a new federal or state budget carved out carefully with a ocalpel. Nor does this change come from a new piece of legislation, such as we had with our hopes wrapped up in a healthcare reform or even the most amazing of candidates. A real change will only come if we can either (a) change our own situation as we read about in all the self-help books or (b) truly change the structure of the systems in which we live. This chapter is about the mindset we need to lead a systematic change to our economy and a structural change in our government; we are talking about making a real difference in every American's life. A change that is almost instant upon signing. To some degree, it is our decision making process that needs to change. A lot of what we see at election time is that our votes are cast with the thought of what someone else might do or with the thought that a vote for one person really means that it will help another candidate. So we must first decide to decide for ourselves. This is the only right you have been given, and with it we can help make a change as we describe in this book. We cannot move forward simply by trying to make a decision for someone else or because we join in some popular opinion.

No individual can give another compassion, this is one emotion that exists within us all; it is simply masked better in some. In fact, we all share the same emotions of pain and joy. It is important to recognize that the emotions we have are the same. It is also important to make note of the fact that we are all very similar on the inside, feeling fear and love. We are far more alike in our psychological makeup, and what we discuss her applies to us all. To exploit one another is not satisfying. To grow as people and as a society, we need to prevent a withering on the vine effect. We have heard songs of revolution and the thought passes through our mind of all the possibilities. We believe that just hearing these words maybe one of our politicians will do something, and we can have a real revolution or perhaps more precisely a society evolution. Then the thought quickly passes as not only impossible and preposterous, but that for our world around us to change into something better for all of us – that God himself will have to come down from parted clouds and make a miracle. To paraphrase Dr. King, it is important to pray and ask for the grace of God, but it does not replace the fact that we must roll up our sleeves and do the work that needs to be done. Maybe something in those songs work for you and me. It was one line that stirred my emotion to stand up and put forth an effort to try. Marvin Gaye sang, "Does anyone really care, who is willing to try, save the children, let's save all the children." Upon hearing these words and feeling them in my heart, I raised my hand and boldly declared that, "I am willing to try." Tommy Silverstein has been in solitary confinement longer than anyone; he embraced art and writing to help pass the time and to some degree it became therapeutic. He wrote clearly what I think is within us all:

"We could be productive citizens, which is all we really wanted from the get go."

While we would like to believe there is opportunity anywhere here in America, the scrolls of failed businesses are also a scroll of broken dreams. These dreams are lined with someone who simply wanted to serve his community. It is time we open the door to man's possibility for being great. In Dr. King's sermon, *The Drum Major Instinct*, he outlines the fact that he who is greatest among us shall be their servant, which means everyone can be great, because everyone can serve. Let us open the door widely for everyone to be great. .Let us learn to embrace the revolution of social change and recognize our similarities as the make-up of people.

PSYCHOLOGY 101

No psychological analysis would be complete without the review of Maslow's hierarchy of needs. From our Psychology 101 class, we learn that before we can think about giving to our community or getting a job; we must first meet the necessities of life to survive: food, water, and shelter. You don't see many homeless people lining up to give. This isn't because of a lack of desire within their hearts; they live with fear of their own survival. What if we could end homelessness, what if as a society we could provide a baseline of survival in helping everyone become better people and give the gifts they were intended to give?

Building on the basic needs, we grow to understand that without a connection to friends and family, we cannot feel good about our self-esteem. We can continue to grow from our self-esteem with our connection to others in hopes of realizing a self-actualization or finding the place we feel we are meant to be making a contribution. Our desire to give, contribute, and serve our fellow man is innate within us. This basic understanding has been accepted since its theoretical introduction in 1943.

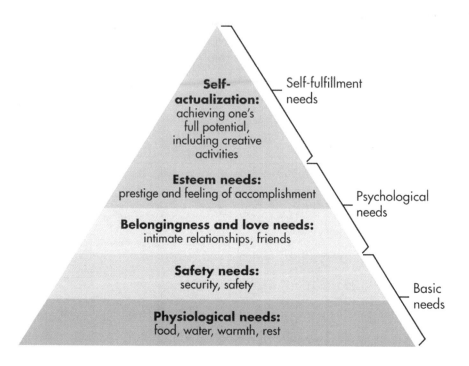

We begin to see the question form quickly: what is a human right? Is water a human right? We have plenty of food to feed the world, should that not be a human right? Police and fire protection, healthcare, shelter, and education for our children, should these be rights? If we the people of the United States can provide for each other basic human rights to remove the fear of survival, then we can help many more people realize self-actualization and greatness. In turn people realize self-actualization by giving to others. It's an investment that spirals for the greater good. If we as a society can ensure basic human rights, then we will naturally make greater connections to our family and community, the truly important parts of life. From our connections, we can be welcomed, feel accepted, and continue to grow into the people we feel we are meant to be. Should air, food, water, healthcare and shelter be a human right when we as a society can provide it for all?

III. BELIEFS

Do we really believe that we can change our society to one based on love? *The fact is that there is a lot of doubt.*

Do we really believe that we can transform our government into an entity that we can not only trust but feel we are a part of? *The fact is that there is a lot of doubt.*

Do we truly believe that we can steer the tanker ship we call our economy off the course of disaster? *The fact is that there is a lot of doubt.*

All of us are skeptical of simply answering yes to any of these questions with the current path that we are on. We have become almost cynical with the notion that real changes like this could occur in our lifetime. The truth is that <u>we are</u> the generation, we cannot afford to wait, and the belief that our children can take care of the debt we are mounting is a huge fallacy. We are the generation, and we are already late in formulating and acting on a new plan that can put us on a different path.

It is easier for us to accept that change will come out of necessity, and that when it absolutely must change is when an alternative path will occur. Without a collapse or devastation, real change in our government, our communities, and our economic system is almost a fantasy. We continue to look for real world solutions, though most of us continue to grow skeptical of the possibilities that we as an average person can make a difference or that real change can occur without a complete catastrophe or an economic meltdown. With a catastrophic change we would be left standing in despair and be forced to create something from fear or become susceptible to change dictated by others out of fear for own future and in hopes that someone can help us.

What if the American economy collapsed? What would be on the other side? To our knowledge and as history as shown us, we only have a handful of choices: communism or dictatorship, anarchism, or some form of socialism. One thing is certain in the wake of failing: there will be a power vacuum and someone thirsty for power will fill it as we will be left in fear of providing for our families.

I believe that right now that we feel within us the confidence that we could and together we actually do have the power to reshape America's destiny. We must realize that we that we have the power to shape a society where we can give each other as citizens basic rights that give us all dignity. We as the people have the power to unite and make changes to create a working government with true leaders where we have a true voice. The truth is that this does not come about by punching out the chard, we can all agree that it is not an election that can make this happen. Just voting for the best candidate will not do it, tax reform is an ugly path that we are currently heading down. Unfortunately, we do not have a national ballot initiative. What we can take confidence in is that we do have a method written in to our Constitution where we the people can influence Constitutional amendments, giving us the power to make real societal changes.

Uniting through the petition process we show our unity to call upon our state legislators to call for a Constitution Convention, while it is the written provision for change the the last Convention was held when it was written.

When united and with specific detail we can make a change aligned with the Lord's prayer or what some might call utopia but nonetheless a societal structure that is more aligned with our natural makeup as human beings.

Believing that there is a way is the first step needed to bring about real social change. We must to crack the door to our mindset of acceptance and begin to accept that there could be a way. There are many theories and there are many beliefs.

Let us begin by recognizing the obvious: that each individual forms his or her own opinion based on his or her own experiences or studies, statistics validating their own truths. While our basic psychological makeup is the same, it is our individual beliefs that truly make us different. It is important to recognize that while it is nice to have someone agree with us, it is also nice to hear another view based on someone else's belief. Through sharing our knowledge, our beliefs and our talents with others we as people learn, grow, and expand our horizons to form new truths.

Let us recognize that different views when connected by the ring of collaboration bring us together with an expanded vision. There is a difference when approaching anything and societal change is not different we must have approach it with love in our heart and we must trust our neighbor and know their heart is the same as ours; it is the power of love that gives us all power.

We are proposing an economic system applied as a structural societal system in which we to monitor each other's contribution much the way you buy or sell something on eBay. The truth is that appreciation for one's work is the carrot that motivates us – think for a second how powerful it is when someone appreciates your work? Conversely taking advantage or not making a contribution when there are opportunities around you everywhere results in we the providers holding the hammer of what to provide someone like that when they come to ask us. However it is the place of appreciation that helps give each purpose. Think how differently the greater majority of workers now feel in the way of their contribution, do you feel that employer/employee appreciation is at high levels

For those that join, for those that contribute we contribute to help make our community and country a beautiful place to be a part of. to keep their vehicle in their lane without error.

It is hard to change a belief. We have only lived with this society, unless you were born abroad, if this is all you know, it's hard to believe that there could be another way. I mean really, the United States of America is the best country on the planet? We seem to win at lots of Olympic events. It's hard to change a belief, but if we think of our beliefs as tables, with the more legs that the table has the more stable that belief will be. If we want to, we can look for methods to support a belief, when you give thought to all of the reasons why you should not smoke for instance; it is easy to see why the belief that you are non-smoker is an easy one. You can apply this technique to any believe including opening yourself up to the idea that our economic system can change.

When we have a new experience or expose ourselves to new information, we take that information and use it to alter or confirm our own beliefs constantly. If we think of our experiences and conscious thoughts as the building blocks that create the legs to our belief tables. It is our collective beliefs make up the person that we are.

It is what we learn and how we chose to interpret that experience or information that makes us individuals. Based on what we form as our beliefs, we will choose what is good or bad, true or false, and this provides the framework for our opinions and convictions about everything. Based on our own experiences, we all will form our own unique view, some of which may be shared with another, and so goes the circle of our experiences, influencing yet helping shape each other as independent thinkers.

Through the experiences that we share together and our interpretations we form our own unique emotional fingerprints, or belief structure. Opening ourselves to learning from others means opening ourselves to collaboration. Opening ourselves to new belief structures expands our thinking forever.

As individuals we must be aware that no one can give us the truth. I or anyone for that matter can give you information, maybe some statistics , but you will take that information and weight it against your believe structure and will always decide what you to believe as truth for you.

When we as individuals believe everything is given to us and that we must live our lives to carry out the tasks assigned, such as a cult or military environment, then we become dangerous. We can even become willing to kill another human being because we are led to believe that the cause is just. Conversely, and yet similarly, this book is attempting to build the pillars within us that will allow us to accept the possibilities of societal change. To believe that it is possible to create a community based on love and harmony and where each of our contributions are valued.

When we suppress our own beliefs and become a tool of a person dictating orders, that's when problems begin. When we stand up and fight for what we believe in we become liberators. This book is asking you to stand up, to provide your ideas, and to take value in your own unique and creative talents and recognize that is through these believes that communities are built.

There are as many belief structures as there are people. The power of religion has shown us that belief has the greatest power of all. Nothing can be accomplished unless someone believes in it first. This is the reason soldiers put their lives at risk; belief is the reason a kamikaze pilot is willing to sacrifice his greatest gift, and belief is the reason why a piece of paper with green ink on it can be exchanged for a gallon of milk. So we must recognize this power of belief and help cross the chasm of possibility and that real societal change is possible. We must belief that we can make a difference, and know that we will be needed and counted on as part of the community and as a citizen of this country no matter where you fit in on the contribution of others. Fundamentally a change such as this we wonder if enough contributing people will come down to the river and help heave sandbags to ensure that the river does not flow over, but let us not forget the people serving in supporting roles all part of the same team whether they drive the sand to the river, help make the bags, or help provide sandwiches for those in the chain – together we all hold value to each other.

IV. LOVE AND FEAR

It is well documented that the power of love is the power for real change – review the lives of Jesus Christ, Martin Luther King, Jr, and Mohandas Gandhi to see what kind of impact love can have when used to help shape or influence society. That is where we want to "come from" within our revolution. Fighting and war does not produce the results of lasting change.

The power to provide confidence and instill positive emotions is what leads us to experience joy. Conversely the power of fear promotes negative or painful emotions. It is our emotions that guide our thinking. It might be obvious, but we move away from painful emotions and towards pleasurable emotions. Sometimes we must go through the pain and sacrifice with the hopes of gaining the pleasure we seek – college is a good example of going through the daily sacrifice to get to a place where you believe will be better. We should recognize that the change described here requires that first we sacrifice. President Clinton summarized it so simply: it is easiest for us to do what we did yesterday. Simply put, change is hard. Fear of crossing a chasm a chasm of the unknown is difficult, and it is especially difficult when you do and you must count on others to come with you. And these others you may not know, these others you may have concern about

180

how they will respond. We will always carry a fear of survival or providing for our families, fear of the unknown and the greatest fear of how others will react to the changes detailed here. So how do we break through the fear? How do we move to a point where we are confident that there is a solution, that all of us will benefit? How do we accept the fact that we will need to work hard, yet smarter and that if we are not serving money our work has purpose and value?

There is a recognition of abundance, not only of what is provided by each of us but of the endless opportunities that will surround us. With our contribution we should know with the societal change we are undertaking and the removal of the need to serve money the rewards are more time doing what matters most and more time with those who matters most.

Anything we do or try is only as good as the individuals involved, but we must look at ourselves and decide for ourselves. We must cast our vote based on how we will act on knowing that we are willing to help our community. We cannot cast our vote based on what we believe others might or might not do. Then together as a general populace of independent thinker we can create change. We the people can assume this responsibility from a handful of political leaders who become hungry for external power and worried about pissing off their campaign contributors and their chance of reelection.

It is the struggle between painful and pleasurable emotion that make it so difficult in many of our inner city streets where opportunities are limited and acceptance is found on the street corner, pleasure is found with drugs, and the joys found from giving are scarce because of the where people are with regards to the concern for basic fears of survival. There have been stories documenting military recruiting that focusing their efforts to fill the required quotas with our youth with limited economical/support. They seek out the hungry, both physically and emotionally, to be a part of something, whether it is gangs, the military, or some other hope of something better.

Moving towards the heart, to live with integrity, wholeness and compassion is how we live in honesty. This correlates to part of what Jesus meant when he suggested knowing the truth and following the inner voice inside that we all know is right. Believing in that inner voice and what we know as right has been one of my life's lessons. Trusting in yourself and your instinct is a confidence and a belief we all have. The adage of the journey from our head to our heart is a big leap, and that journey should be supported within the community if we are to live and give of ourselves from our hearts. Having confidence in ourselves and in our own inner voice is what opens us up the possibility of living in a community of love, a community where each of us has self-worth.

It is the ability to live with truth and compassion and to love from your heart that continues to open up the fields of possibilities. Living with anger and fear limits our abilities and our opportunities to make a positive impact in our community. That is why we grow fearful when the opportunities for us to make a living and provide for ourselves and our families are limited. The ability to make a positive impact becomes much more difficult because of the burden of concern that we carry. Unfortunately, our current economic system is based on fear and not love. It is fear that if I give my pelt of fur for the betterment of the community it might not be reciprocated as the pair of shoes that I may need. This method in which we reward the values of contribution has manifested itself into a world where 60% of people live below the poverty line, American financial institutions are on the brink of ruin, 46 of our 50 states are operating in the red, individual pension funds are at risk, schools and community centers face closures, and in general, we are forced to try to do more with less. This is all because our economic system will not support us, and not because there are not enough raw materials or people willing to help. This all stems from a fear-based system versus one rooted in love. Think for a minute about anything you approach,, and what the outcomes like when you approach something with fear versus love and trust. Our system is not without trust. You must trust the person or company you're doing business with or you simply won't want to do business with that person or company. You must trust the piece of paper you're given for your contribution and that it can be traded for another man's goods or service that you may need or want. Without trust and confidence in each other and a belief that the pieces of paper have value our current economic system collapses. So let's take note of that trust that we have for each other.

Whether it is anger at the world, our circumstances, or at performance in the face of expectations we must become aware of the pain that is produced by fear and doubt. From there, we must move away from this pain toward the spirit of love and trust, and in this way, we open ourselves up to an empowerment, a peace within ourselves and an acceptance towards others. We open ourselves up the possibility of creating and being a part of an accepting community and united country.

Our ability to experience any situation with love and trust while being void of fear and doubt removes all the painful emotions that could otherwise be produced and limiting our potential. Capturing the power of love and trust is at the heart of this plan; we must root any call for social change with love and trust for it to truly be successful and accepted. Not only that, but creating communities based on love, acceptance and an appreciation is at the root of the change we have been calling for.

It is this trust in one another and appreciation for each other's unique contribution on this planet that, if allowed, will foster a love of community and an acceptance that we all long for. We already have this trust, but fully bringing this into our consciousness opens us up to changing our world into something amazingly beautiful. Using this power of choice to use fear and doubt or love and trust can have profound effects on the control of your emotions. If you think of your body and spirit as a processor of the energy of our experiences, the power to make a painful emotion is within you just as much as the power to create a joyful experience. Think of all energy that flows into you as pure and wholesome or the experiences that we have simply presented at face value. It is our choice of interpretation. We all know we cannot change people or circumstances. You can only change the way in which you process your experiences. The choice you make as a spiritual being is to process any experience with love and trust or fear and doubt. The outcome is either joyful or painful. Anger, jealousy, appreciation, joy, gratitude, they are all information that help us understand what our fears are and where we are with love, all tied to our belief structure. The truth is all emotions should be experienced with gratitude; they provide us with information about ourselves. This describes a spiritual experience we all encounter on a continual basis. The notion and plan presented here is presented from the ultimate love. It is intended to be received with love for all mankind and a trust that, we as Americans have the resources, the wherewithal, and the willingness to begin with a sort of sacrifice for the good of all mankind.

The pursuit of external power to manipulate and control others is what leads us as kids to fight over a car in the sandbox. It is also that same pursuit that has littered our history with wars, crisis, conflicts, and a massive amount of deaths with our sons and daughters (it has been reported that over 600,000 Iraqis have died since 2003 alone – start adding that to the World Wars, Vietnam, Korea, or go back even further), the death toll in a struggle for power is profound. If you read the headlines or watch a news broadcast, then it appears that conflict is past, present and our future. Simply try to make a friend do something they do not want to do and continue to persist, and then you will understand completely the struggle for power over one another does not make for real change compared to the virtues of listening, understanding, collaborating, and living in harmony. Compare the war fought in Iraq to the liberation led by Gandhi, and we see the contrast of real change where united love overcomes fear. War does not shed light on wrong doings. We all need to understand the need for war if we are truly fighting for love and peace, but does it not make sense for our leaders to sit down at the table of understanding? Ghandi and Dr. King, lead movements based on love and they were able to change the way we think, and make accepted, real, lasting societal change without resorting to violence. Though they did receive blows, unfortunately the fight they fought the blows in which they received was a method of showing the injustice.

However the accomplishments of Gandhi and Dr. King were not realized by succumbing to fear. They were not fearful of sitting down at the negotiation table, not fearful or pursuing something that may have been considered going against the socially accepted norm, even against the law at the time.

186

While our country may have been founded based on a freedom, based on we the people being active in our government, most were created based on a conquest or out of ruin. But the truth is no matter the government structure the underlying economic system used is nevertheless based on a fear. Our founding fathers architected the government of United States based on a desire to create something better and with the idea that it should reinvent itself to serve the growing and changing needs of the people. Somewhere we have lost the boldness required of reinventing our government and have let corporate interests reshape it.

Now we have lost the trust in our own government. We not only downplay the notion of "By the People, For the People," but we almost dismiss it as a once-upon-a-time fallacy. We now buy into the political rhetoric at election time. The type of rhetoric that claims this candidate can truly provide change, or the opponent will bring ruin. But soon after every election, our fears grow that real change will really never occur. We grow scared that we will only create when it becomes absolutely necessary, out of ruin or devastation. The truth is underneath the desire for change is a fear that out of this devastation or collapse we have no idea what a required change might look like other than what history has shown us which is that we are susceptible to dictatorship or some form or governmental socialism. Using the power of love and trust and basing a society in this same spirit, we can provide a change for the good, open ourselves up to more opportunity than we can imagine, and unburden ourselves like nothing else could.

It is at the core of what we all want, yet we fear that it is impossible, unobtainable, or that others would take advantage of a loving, caring society, we need to let go of the fear and open ourselves up to a trust of one another, this is at the root.

We need to first open ourselves with a loving heart and believe that we can create a society based on welcoming and accepting communities. We must begin by believing and trusting that real change is possible and from there you can make the decision that what is being proposed here would be a society that you would want to be a part of and that you would be willing to contribute to. If you find this in your heart, we can continue to share the possibilities and look what love and trust can do when we spread it across our country.

V. SUMMARY

We not only must be ready in our heads for social change, but we also must be prepared in our hearts. During the Olympics, Tom Brokaw shared a story of how the community came together in Newfoundland during the 9/11 tragedy where they received every inbound international plane on that day. Remember how the entire country was ready to do anything for each other on the day after the shock of that tragedy? In Newfoundland, people were making their homes available to perfect strangers; they were making food for them, and do you know what happened? Through that act of kindness all kinds of lifelong friendships were created. I remember stories of citizenship from my home town of Cedar Rapids, Iowa, when the Cedar River, which runs through the middle of town, rose to a severe flood stage in 2008. Downtown was under 10 feet of water for weeks. It is documented that officials were amazed at the amount of people that came down to help. There were literally hundreds of people helping to save other people, simply willing to help anyway they could.

The social change described here starts with confidence in each other. If your community or country needed you, the truth is there will be enough like-minded individuals willing to help, it is our nature and we have seen it time and time again. To make this change work, America will have to be self-sufficient in the goods and services we as Americans provide. Under this economic system proposal, we will only have what we can make in America, we need to be prepared to be thrifty, we need to be ready to reuse and fix first not dispose first. If we can have faith in each other, then we can build a bridge of trust back to our government and correct the problems associated with our current economic system.

We do have the power to forgive our debts and debtors, our trespasses and trespassers, and we can ensure each of us have our daily bread, and we can create a kingdom here on earth, and we will give all of the glory to our children, as we were taught when Jesus walked the earth.

Amen

Chapter 6 Great Teachings

If we look at some of the great teachers and philosophers throughout history, we will see how their messages connect with what is being presented here and can be incorporated into a systemic change for a new society. In looking to create a social change, we must consider the great minds, a few of the greatest ideas, the greatest philosophies, and the great social change architects that ever walked this planet, including Jesus Christ, Henry David Thoreau, Martin Luther King Jr., and Mahatma Gandhi. We will see how their teachings overlap in substance with each other and how they are used in the architecture of government and the economic system proposed here.

When applying these teachings to society in a way that we may have only been imagined, we must first realize that within our hands lies the possibility to transform the United States of America into the drum major of love from a world currently filled with power struggles.

Using these teachings might be the easiest place for us to come together. We are already familiar with many of them, and we can agree with much of what we already know from their teachings, as they've been a long been a part of not only our history but our hope. These teachings are almost accepted as common sense. I believe that most of what we learn from these great teachers is accepted with a sense of logic that our society should be more aligned with the Lord's prayer for example but the problem is we simply have never believed that as a culture we could create something of that magnitude, without some sort of an unimaginable coup or divine intervention.

To start, let's address the issue of religion. What we are proposing is to design a society based on many of the teachings you would find in many religions, and we are referencing Jesus Christ. Whether you believe that he died on the cross for our sins or not, his teachings hold a lot of universal truths and valuable lessons. We can agree with many of the truths in the Ten Commandments, and you find much of his teachings inspiring other amazing social change architects, such as Gandhi and Dr. King.

We shall appreciate their teachings much in the way that our teachers have taught us that $2 + 2 = 4$. By our acknowledgement of the truths of the man's teaching and our reference to a universal God, no matter the name, we can find a common ground and a common sense approach in the way we could and should interact with each other.

Our first point of common sense and acknowledgement is the power of the people; if we can all operate from the same page, as proposed here, then we can create a non-violent revolution as is outlined within our Constitution and has been shown to us by history's greatest minds. We know that when united, the power of the people can do anything. So let us look at some of these teachings and apply them to what is being proposed here in this book.

Jesus Christ

From the teachings of Jesus Christ and the messages that he brought, it only makes sense to ask the question what would Jesus do (WWJD)? How would Jesus want us to live if we were to give consideration to his teachings in the way we govern or provide for ourselves? What would Jesus say about the design of a working economic system? I am only asking for consideration here, and that we comfortably shine the light on this question so that we open ourselves up to an understanding of his teachings not life after death religious beliefs.

That preceding concept alone shows the stark contrast of our current domestic and world economic crisis. It sheds light on how we deny ourselves from the abundance that surrounds us and how may have lost touch with the lesson of, "he is who is greatest among us shall be the servant". The question also shows the possibilities of love and how the structure of our society, the way we work with each other in an effort to serve one another, is restricted because of the necessity to earn a living. The love and desire that is naturally within all of us is a bit disconnected because of our needs to survive. The US Government and the teachings of Christ, while once may have based on a in God we trust principle now continues to drift farther apart in an effort not to offend someone. Compound this with the cutthroat world capitalism has created, and we find a chasm between the societal structure and that which was taught by Christ.

We understand somewhat the theory of separation of church and state, but church and economics – well, that sounds like an evangelist out there trying to sell tickets. Jesus and economics seem like oil and water to me, but let's take a look at what Jesus would do. Clearly we address the notion that Jesus would not draw up on paper an economic system that promotes greed and fear. As Christians, or simply believers in a God, do we believe that Jesus would endorse capitalism as a good idea? With over half the world living in poverty, debt, and children starving when there is plenty of food to feed the world, it seems obvious that we've proven this isn't the case. Furthermore, promoting competition over collaboration isn't at all what Jesus was about. No, I doubt very seriously that Jesus would approve of our current economic system and capitalism in general. If we sought His approval to continue on this path, do you think it possible that he would sign his name to approve it? Would he say, "Yes, continue on this road? Well done my children." Or do we believe that he might be able to enlighten us and offer us an alternate way of thinking and do you think we would have the courage to follow it? Consider the red words provided in the bible and the depiction of the way he lived his life, and make the decision for yourself.

If we listen in on Dr. King as he teaches about the bible's Drum Major Instinct, we hear the competitive nature of: "I must be first, I must be supreme, and I must rule the world." We see his view applied as personal, as a country's nature of military supremacy, and even as it relates to the competition necessary in capitalism. Dr. King continues his teaching of the Drum Major Instinct of wanting to be great and supreme in describing Jesus response to his followers, "You want to be first? You want to be great? You want to be important? You want to be significant? Well you ought to be, he preaches is as is Jesus' response, these are good instincts to have if you use them correctly, but I want you to be first in love, first in generosity." When Jesus spoke to his disciples James and John on this very subject he said, "I can't make you great, and really I can't make you first. You must earn it, and you must be prepared. For it is he who is greatest among that shall be your servant." With that, a new definition of "greatness" is born. With that, we remember Jesus washing the feet of his followers as one who tried to serve. And with that definition of greatness, Reverend King points out, we can all be great because we can all serve. Let us all be Drum Majors for greatness in the way we serve other in love and in generosity.

Within this, we can all live with abundance. Addressing our fears that in a system where all we have is what is available to us and we can take comfort in the fact that what we need will be provided. Let us remember the words of Jesus as he addresses the need to worry about what will be provided, "Do the birds forage and store food?" Look at the birds flying through the air. They do not plant gardens for food, nor do they gather the seeds they eat. Our heavenly Father feeds them, and they do not worry that they will have enough to eat.

Conversely, the monetary system does not ensure that we will have enough to eat. It is our trust in each other, it is our trust in God, and it is our absolute knowledge that together all things are possible. We all know that there is enough food we all are aware of what is simply thrown away if it is not sold, and that truth be told if more was needed, more food could be produced. It is not the monetary system that ensures we are all fed. Actually, it is quite the opposite; the staggering numbers of those that go hungry do so not because there is enough provided, it is because of the restrictions of the economic system.

Money does not guarantee that there will be enough. On the contrary, it is teaching us to do with less and less as we face the reality of inflation and the continual cutting of budgets.

> Luke 16:13,
> You cannot serve both God and money.

Henry David Thoreau

Written in 1849, Thoreau's essay *Civil Disobedience* has been the source of reference for not only Gandhi and Dr. King, but it was the reference for a number of movements for social change including: :the 1940s Danish resistance to German occupation; in the 1950s it was valued for those Americans that opposed McCarthyism's; it was influential in the 1960s with the struggle of the South African apartheid; and in the 70s it was rediscovered by anti-war activists. Now it is our turn to use these teachings and to open our minds to the possibility of creating an effective change for the equality of man.

> *"When men are prepared for it, that will be the kind government which they will have."*

> Henry David Thoreau

This quote was taken out of context and for good reason, preceding that quote it is written in Thoreau's essay; "That government is best which governs not at all." I do not believe anarchy makes sense. Having a stoplight at a busy intersection might make more sense, unless a roundabout can be put in place and we can all continue moving in harmony. The quote by itself it does put things into perspective: that we are not untethered buoys carried by the waves of fate. We can create social change, but we have to make sense to ourselves, we must be readied for it, and it must work within the harmony of time to be effective. Within the context of which Thoreau uses this opening quote, I must disagree with his theory that a government that governs not at all is somehow good. It makes social sense to have a structure in place that serves the people as a functioning government, for things like roads, police services, education, water, and medicine to name a few essential human rights. If unshackled from an ever shrinking budget, government's sole purpose of building the best community, county, state, and country possible is noble.

Those that get into politics to serve their neighbors or fellow countryman have nobility. Can we blame the corruption that we experience on the systems? Yes, yes we can, we see it clearly with professional athletes who have no loyalty to a team, and they look at only the opportunity to provide for themselves and their children. It is the same with politicians and the temptation to accept the influence of money – which most must do if they want to stay in office.

Thoreau refers to the men who stand up for our country as the army needed to defend its borders. These are the farmers, doctors, and blacksmiths that took up a musket and first fought off outside influence to create our United States of America, and we have forever tried to capture that spirit of freedom within our American borders. We should recognize the bravery that exists and reaches to every corner of country and within every large and small town. When we are awaken and are made aware, as experienced in the lessons of flight 93, there is bravery among us and we will act, we will be ready to lay our lives down to save others.

Having arrived at our present day, we continue to recognize the bravery of our citizens with the men and women that make up our fighting armies, our first responders, the nurses in an emergency room, the truth is bravery is all around us. Those that fight on our behalf will always deserve our deepest appreciation, but let us not forget the connection of the supporting "ground crew" that also deserves our appreciation. As Dr. King eloquently put it in his Nobel Peace Prize acceptance speech, you honor the known pilot, but it takes a team on the ground to make a successful journey possible. So, in our appreciation we shall not forget that we work together for the common goals.

The economic system proposed here is built on our appreciation for one another, in recognizing your contribution. I will help if I am in a position to help, and altruistically it is my desire to do so. Henry David Thoreau's teachings go on to illustrate our common desires of unlocking the ability of government to act swiftly through the steps of progress, for its defense and its management of resources and manpower. With the Constitutional amendments proposed here allowing the people to become their own House of Representatives and playing an active role in our government through our own personal computers or interactive televisions, we are ready, and we can have that type of government. When technology is used properly, we have the keys to unlock such a system where our voice has value. Our communication system gives us this ability to instantly tabulate votes, oversee and share resources, identify needs, make for distribution of goods. Couple this with our ability to mass produce almost anything, and we can see that have been given a chance to have a huge impact and respond almost immediately to the needs of our countrymen, much in the way we respond to the rivers bank of an impending flood in a swift manner.

We have a lot to be grateful for in the way of our talented men and women of America and across the world. Let us remember our communication system, the World Wide Web, and how it was created by Tim Berners-Lee and given freely to the public without the infringement of his due copyright privileges. This altruistic spirit of giving for the good of mankind is a beautiful light that we all can enjoy. Mr. Thoreau points to the matter in which the government forces its will on us and how we as a people can expect the taxation on our wealth. Interpreted from the statement, "Governments show thus how successfully men can be imposed on, even impose on themselves, for their own advantage." It seems that the weight of our tax burden is heavy, and it is the notion of taxes that strike a real nerve with us. The taxation notion is ever increasing, and judging from the past campaigns it is the candidate that says he/she will not raise taxes that maintains his or her his chance of winning. Stating they will raise our taxes works as an instant defeat button. So how would it feel to remove the burden of taxation? We must remember that though we remove the burden of taxes, we must bear the weight of the actual work needed to provide for ourselves as a country. We must be confident that there are brave men and women to help protect our citizens, our borders, and our children as we have seen throughout history. We must feel confident that a community can come together to build housing much in the way we see on TV's makeover shows, and we must be confident that we will see the beauty of man's spirit as they join together to help one another.

It is good for us to remember Thoreau's teachings, and specifically that the government did not settle the West. It does not educate, it does make the sick person well, and contrary to some thinking, it did not create the internet. It is individuals within our nation that make things happen or not happen. It is good for us as citizens to remember that the Constitution begins, "We the people..." It is a document that we have agreed on as the basis for our laws, and it gives a needed framework for our society. Overall, it is a good thing. The document is something the people say OK to, not any one branch of government, not a crew of judges, but "We the people" agree that this is the government we want. We do not deny the fact that someone must write it, but if we do not like it, then we shall express our frustrations, we shall create a movement with purpose until we feel that our liberties and freedoms that are our God given rights are ours once again.

Remember that it is us, the United People of America, that can change the government all at once with perfect timing. If first we seek to answer what kind of government we would like, when we are ready, that will be what we have. Thoreau goes on to remind us that the rule of democracy is majority, and if we as a people can vote with our conscience and the ability to move swiftly, then that shall be the best government.

Thoreau's essay goes on to points to some of the greatest problems within our government. He reminds us that corporations do not have a conscience, but a corporation of conscientious men is a corporation with a conscience. He brings up a good point that it is the men and women that make up the self-interest of corporate America.

However, today it is corporations that have grown and have now become unbridled in their ability to influence government policy, which is frightening because the truth is the aim of a corporation is to increase profits and to serve its own self interests. The current economic climate has brought about fear for survival and a systematic structure that promotes self-interests. While it is illustrated under the limelight of corporate greed, it also becomes clear in professional sports where we as fans would like to be reminded of loyalty and team. However, that notion is a bygone of looking out for one's own security. This coupled with the firings that seem to come so easily, professional sports provides a mirror of a society with a disposable worker workplace. The greater majority of players eligible for a big contract justify it by recognizing the nature of the free market, business climate of "it's just business," and the notion that if they don't look out for themselves, the owners sure as hell will be looking out for themselves. Therefore selfishness must take precedence.

Pause for a second to think how sad it is that our society has come to serve each other in this manner. On the subject of corporations, it is worth noting that, given our current climate in which our government has given our corporations first amendment rights and unlimited influence with the money they have, we are giving the elite few (1% of the population) more rights than the majority because of their means to introduce and promote legislation, manipulate the media and influence the mindset of the populace.

But united we can take this back. United we have a voice so large it trumps all power of money and power of the great influencers. All it takes is the power of individual thinking versus controlled thinking. We can recognize and appreciate the fact that our men and women of the armed forces stand up and are willing to sacrifice everything so that we may have it all. But in his essay, Thoreau makes the point that these mass of men become machines with their bodies, and in most cases there is no ability to exercise free judgment or moral sense. If we look at the trials of Nuremberg, we realize that there is a line between what is being asked of us versus the right to differentiate between what we know as right or wrong. In their case it is a military order, but we can certainly draw a parallel to that of us as citizens and what that government and media does to steer our consciousness.

Thoreau goes on to address the legislators, politicians, lawyers, and office-holders serving the state chiefly with their heads and rarely making any moral distinctions. They are likely to serve the devil without intending to he goes on to say. Do we believe that the men and women pulling the trigger and dodging bullets from both sides of a war would rather there be a different way? Gandhi suggests that peace can be found at the table of understanding if it is supported with a willingness to believe that an acceptable compromise can be made. Let us recognize the value in Thoreau's words as advocates for our own values: "A wise man will only be useful as a man, and not submit to be clay, and stop a hole to keep the wind away."

Addressing the right of a revolution, his details include the barrier for such which was broken in 1775 when Americans, before they knew they were citizens of a republic, fought for independence in Concord and Lexington. Eloquently, he writes that all machines (referring to government) have their friction (referring to business or the 1% of influence). When friction comes to have its own machine and oppression and robbery are organized, we should all say, "Let us not have such a machine any longer!" We must not only cry out but take action when 99% of a nation's population has been undertaken to the refuge of slaves, and a whole country is unjustly overrun, in our case by corporate interest, and subjected to the influence of big money. It is not too soon for honest men to rise up, revolutionize, and make the world of haves, of possibility, of harmony, and of acceptance within a community.

Unjust laws exist, and as Gandhi says, as there are unjust men. In support or not support, Thoreau's *Civil Disobedience* essay makes an interesting note of man's duty and honor. The beauty of the solution described here is that it would precipitate a system that promotes giving and not greed, producing far less unjust men working together to make society a better place – this is the catalyst of change being proposed here.

Government should anticipate and provide for reform, encouraging its citizens to point out faults. How else can we learn and become better without ideas and different points of view? Throughout the essay, Thoreau strikes thought provoking chords of civil awareness, such as, "One would think that a deliberate and practical denial of the government's authority was the only offense never contemplated by government." Mr. Thoreau points to the Government's injustice as a friction and the approach of doing nothing that perchance the friction caused will wear smooth or the machine will simply wear out. However, if the system requires that we be an agent of injustice to ourselves, our family, or to another, then we must break the law. We must let our life be a counter friction to stop the machine. Though we have seen this with even with the life of Christ, where some accused him of breaking the law of that time, Gandhi and Dr. King were imprisoned because they were viewed as something other than good law abiding citizens. It should be pointed out that the change we are asking for here simply asks for your support in the way of a signed petition, possibly your help and an acceptance of possibility. We want this change to work in harmony with the law, in harmony with the Constitutional means for true social change, it does require breaking an unjust law or being imprisoned.

It is very interesting how Thoreau describes the way the change starts. He gives an example of slavery that was still the norm a mere 150 years ago (nearly 100 years after the Constitution was signed slavery was still legal). Thoreau notes if one thousand, if one hundred, if ten men whom we knew – if ten honest men, if one honest man ceasing to hold slaves were to actually withdraw from co-partnership and be locked up in the county jail, it would be the abolition of slavery in America. The truth is the truth, and sometimes we simply need to shine the light on injustice so that we can simply see it and stir the consciousness that exists in us all. When Dr. King's civil rights demonstration in Birmingham was met with the police turning fire-hoses on the crowd, the rest of the world could see clearly the injustice and that, as a society with a conscience, this is not the way we treat people.

With regards to the catalyst for revolution, Thoreau makes the point of our current state of public political involvement with the question, "How can a man be satisfied to entertain an opinion if his opinion is aggrieved?" We hear political opinion all around us. Is it a growing trust in our government? Is there a sense of empowerment or distrust and disconnect? He furthers his point with the notion of the wise use of our tax dollars with the question, "If you are cheated out of a single dollar by your neighbor, you do not rest satisfied with knowing that you are cheated." It is time we not rest knowing that we have been cheated and our voices are drowned by the influences of corporate interests regardless of the administration.

Dr. Martin Luther King, jr

A minority is powerless while it conforms to the majority.

If a man hasn't discovered something he will die for, he isn't fit to live.

Dr. Martin Luther King

Time and time again Dr. King called on us to "question the capitalistic economy" and "restructure America." He raised the questions like "Who owns the oil? Who owns the water? Who owns the air?" Dr. King was taken from us as he began to assemble his third movement, a movement of economic reform.

He opened our eyes and changed the world forever, he helped change the way we view each other to the point that we recognize the content of character rather than money or skin color. After being introduced as the Moral Leader of the Nation, when he gave his "I Have a Dream" speech, he stood up once again to the morality of Vietnam War. In 1968, five years after taking on equality and standing up to the President of the United States to publicly denounce the morality of the Vietnam War, he was tackling the issue of joblessness and economic deprivation.

Dr. King's proposed economic solution took the form of a guaranteed income. While the solutions presented by Dr. King are very different than what is being proposed here, the outcomes of dignity are similar. The Poor People's Campaign was never realized and was thrown into disarray when Martin Luther King, Jr., was assassinated on April 4, 1968, just weeks before the campaign was set to commence.

It should be stated that 40 years later, our perspective has changed immensely. We see and understand the messages he was able to share with both equality and the light shed on an unjust war. Not only do we see that he was right, but we honor him with a memorial in Washington, D.C., and federal holiday celebrating his birth.

Unfortunately, we did not get to fully see the message tied to the Poor People's Campaign. The campaign still had roots as Presidential hopeful Robert Kennedy was becoming an ever more resolute voice for economic justice. However, just two months after King's assassination, so would follow the Kennedy's own assassination. Since then, the movement for a basic economic security for all never again gained momentum. Dr. King argued in one of his last sermons, "If a man does not have a job or an income, he has neither life nor liberty nor the possibility for the pursuit of happiness, he merely exists." He made these arguments when America was going through one of the greatest periods of economic expansion in our country's history. So, how might this argument be received now amidst an economic crisis as our government goes through a period of austerity on the road to a possible collapse?

In 1956, while studying at the Crozer Theological Seminary, King presented concepts such as an imaginary letter from the apostle Paul to American Christians, which stated, "Oh America, how often we have taken necessities from the masses to give luxuries to the classes. God never intended for one group of people to live in superfluous inordinate wealth, while other live abject deadening poverty." To those of us who still do not believe in the validity of the campaign, of its effectiveness, or its ability to make true economic change, Dr. King argued otherwise. He explained, "Two years before we went into Selma, the Civil Rights Commission recommended that something be done in a very strong manner to eradicate discrimination, yet nothing was done until we mounted a movement and really engaged in action geared toward moving the nation away from the course it was following." Injustice anywhere is a threat to justice everywhere he stated on many occasion. For King, there was no path to just economic policy except for organizing and appealing to the conscience and the self-interest of the nation. On April 4, 1968, in room 306 of the Lorraine Motel, Dr. King was working on his sermon titled *Why*

American May Go to Hell for the following Sunday. His focus was taking a change of course from civil rights to anti-war and populist economics. His murder on that day left his plans for a massive Poor People's Campaign in disarray. Some claim that his assassination was the result of his new stance against the war and the notion of economic reforms. "They" feared King might topple the "power structure" and that is one theory on what had him killed. The last week of his life, Dr. King struggled with what to do next. He preached, "We must turn a minus into a plus, a stumbling block into a steppingstone – we must move on." Fifty years later, I believe Dr. King would still be fighting for equality and be an advocate for the poor, unemployed, and those that are losing their homes in foreclosure. It is time that we pick up where Dr. King left off, embrace the notion of equality, take a stance in the name of true economic reform, and pave the way for every man, women, and child to walk in the light of creative altruism. It is time we start letting love make the world go around, not money.

Mahatma K. Gandhi

"If humanity is to progress, Gandhi is inescapable. He lived, thought, acted, and inspired the vision of humanity evolving toward a world of peace and harmony."

Dr. Martin Luther King

210

How could a meek and fragile person inspire millions to bring about a profound change in a way the mightiest with swords had never achieved before? When we look at the fight to regain self-rule for India by removing the instilled British power, and we barely believe it possible that one man, one set of ideals, proved to be more powerful than tanks, bombs, and armies of men with machine guns. It was one man rising up with love and a new concept of non-violence that not only showed to everyone a government system of oppression but united his fellow citizens to join in the struggle to "overthrow" an instilled government. Through his actions he was able to show clearly the injustice of racial and economic oppression. Through his actions, even his imprisonment he placed the design and control back to the natives of India. He led them on a path of peaceful demonstration to having self-rule and all of the positives and negatives that come along with that.

> *"Power is of two kinds. One is obtained by the fear of punishment and the other by acts of love. Power based on love is a thousand times more effective and permanent then the one derived from fear of punishment."*

> **Mahatma K. Gandhi**

Gandhi taught us that we can bring harmony to our world by becoming champions of love and peace for all. Bringing about peace through non-violence, through Gandhi's example we awake each day with the following resolve:

I shall not fear anyone on Earth.

I shall fear only God.

I shall not bear ill will toward anyone.

I shall not submit to injustice from anyone.

I shall conquer untruth by truth and in resisting untruth.

I shall put up with all suffering.

In his struggle to fight against the British reign, his message was as transparent to his enemy as it was to his followers. He proved that we can bring about world peace by seeking and pursuing truth for the benefit of mankind. We can resolve the greatest of our differences if we dare to have a constructive conversation with our enemy.

In the Old Testament, Joseph the interpreter of dreams, was rejected by his brothers, but ultimately saved them. Jesus was rejected by his own religion and crucified in the name of blasphemy. Nelson Mandela was imprisoned and isolated for nearly 28 years before being released and awarded his prize for peace. Dr. King was attacked and jailed by the government that ultimately recognized him with his own holiday. Gandhi was imprisoned and killed by the merciless, those that were simply were ignorant to his message and the man he was. Standing up for what is right is not necessarily received well at the time.

Time has a way of changing perspective, and their bravery for standing up for what is right earned them all honor in our history for helping make the world a better place. Gandhi used non-violence to transform the minds of a nation and the world.

On April 6, 1930, after having marched 241 miles on foot from village to the sea, he arrived at the coastal village and gathered salt. He openly defied the British Salt Law. Within a month, people all over India were making salt illegally, and more than 100,000 were sent to jail. Many fell victim to police violence, but none retaliated or even defended themselves. This simple act exposed the injustice of British rule and was a vital step towards India's independence. Shedding the light on injustice is at the root of effective non-violent protest. Gandhi firmly believed that if violence was used to achieve any end – even if it was employed in the name of justice – the result would be more violence. Instead, he led the fight with what he called "soul-force" or the "the power of truth," meaning to stand firmly behind one's ideas without hatred toward the opposition. Civil disobedience and non-cooperation may mean breaking a specific law and then facing the consequences. Let us all open ourselves to the spirit of non-violence.

Another element of effective non-violence is non-cooperation; this tactic need not break any law, but simply pull out all support for an unjust system. We see that attempt with the Occupy Wall Street demonstrations, where they ask people to move their money from banks to a credit union. Breaking an unjust law in an effort to shine a light of an unjust system might be exactly what a society needs to see before making any real change. Gandhi organized such non-cooperation after the British army massacred 400 unarmed demonstrators. Withdrawing support for the British administrators, they ground to a halt the massive machine of an unjust government.

Mohandas K. Gandhi has been given the title of the "Great Soul," and he transcended religions and his teachings of non-violence have been reincarnated in many movements. They have shown us the way of living in peace, and they have provided for us a method of change far more powerful than bombs and guns. He has shown us the power of love and trust in our fellow man. On January 28, 2008, Jesse Jackson delivered the Gandhi Memorial Lecture in Delhi. He made the note of Dr. King's referral to the Drum Major Instinct and dreamers who marched to a different beat and heard a different sound. They were often considered counterculture or swimming upstream. Dreamers are sometimes called misfits, but they are the agents of change. These types of dreamers are not asleep; they dream with their eyes open. There are many philosophies and leaders of change that have had profound social impact, and though we may have just touched the essence of their impact, hopefully we have shown their influences on the plan presented within this book.

I recognize that on the surface this plan might be considered radical, but the truth of the matter is that this proposal taps into our innate desires and gives a chance for our love to conquer fear. This plan lays out the framework needed to create a society that provides for each other a baseline of human rights to be provided to where all of us know that air, water, shelter, food, healthcare, and safety. These rights as a basic human need are provided for our own basic dignity. Providing for each other these basic needs, we give everyone a chance at greatness in their ability to serve.

This plan illuminates a different path and provides for an Amended Constitution to change an American society to thrive and prosper no matter the despair that may be caused by a manmade or natural disaster. This plan wipes out any effects of an economic recession, depression, or even what some may say is an unsustainable economic system headed for cataclysmic ends. Opening the method, where we can serve one another, we can all be great in our country, the United States of America.

Chapter 7   A Different American History

How can you buy or sell the sky, the warmth of the land?
The idea is strange to us.
If we do not own the freshness of the air and the sparkle of the water, how
can you buy them?
Every part of this earth is sacred to my people.

Chief Seattle

America already had a culture when Columbus landed. Unfortunately, as Europeans continued to come to the new world, they sought ways to instill a societal structure that they knew instead of understanding and learning the ways of living in harmony in a sacred circle, like those that already lived here before it was "discovered".

There are plenty of stories about the conflict brought upon by the white man's conquest, the broken treaties, the forcing of tribes off their lands to designated reservations, and how the balance became upset. However, it is not easy to find the story of the Native Americans before the landing of Columbus. While the Indian people have tried to maintain their identity and culture, a lot of it has been lost to the story of struggle and conquest. This chapter takes time to look at an American history where the societal structure was different.

In proposing a systemic change to our societal structure, it is important for us to understand and to look at the way different societies function. Hopefully by opening our eyes we open ourselves up to new possibilities. America is great because there is a freedom to choose, but the way in which we live within the current economic and government systems leaves us all desiring change. It is time we step outside of the rhetoric and open ourselves to walking a different path, but let us first look at what some other paths look like to see if we can gain insight to what we might like to see.

We know that socialist systems and other countries function differently, and we can benefit from understanding that there is a lot of good to be learned from almost any community. In Australia, for instance, the country's original inhabitants, the Aboriginal and Torres Strait Islanders, are the custodians of one of the world's oldest continuing cultures.

What we want to do is look at how America functioned before the European influence. How did the original inhabitants live in harmony with our Mother Earth? How did they pay respect to each other, and how did they appreciate everything and everyone that contributed to the community? The Native American community lived with humor. Living in a sacred manner is not to live in solemn self-denial but to take pleasure in being alive in the world.

It has been argued that when Columbus landed and encountered what we now know as American Indians, he wrote in his journal that he had encountered people of God ("una geste in dios"). That the "in dios" which is the basis for the label Indian as opposed to what some may say he thought he landed in India.

We are all too familiar with the struggles faced by the Indians as the settlers fought to take over their land, forcing them west until they did not have any further west to go. These struggles and interruption of the sacred way included the buying of land, which did not make sense to the Indian way of life, and even having this government banning their dances for generations. Let us look at that life in hopes that we open ourselves up to realizing alternative ways in which society can function.

Symbolism

The number 4 represents completeness. It can be related to the directions, it can be related to colors - white, black, yellow, and red - and even the representation of the people of the world. All colors of people together creating one culture, coming from the one spirit. Considering that there is but one spirit, we are all part of the same world (or planetary community). We cannot change the colors, just our attitude towards all living things on the planet. I don't mean just the two-legged creatures, but the four legged kinds, the winged kind, those in the water, and those that crawl. Focusing our attention on what we have in common, we may find that we are all brothers and sisters, and we need this relationship to thrive in this universe.

218

The Sacred Hoop represents the circle of all life, the four directions, the Earth, and everything that lives. Everything is related. This symbolism recognizes that our existence is intertwined and that our survival depends upon maintaining a balanced relationship with everything to keep the hoop connected. It goes even deeper than that by recognizing this relationship. Within the hoop it recognizes that we are all united as relatives. They that live with this philosophy go so far as to say your problems are my problems. When the sacred hoop is intact, then we all feel safe. Our society is today is more "every man for himself" and "survival of the fittest," and we recognize that the circle does not play a part in our broken society limping due to man's disregard for his fellow man, the Earth, and those that live upon her. When we deviate from the teachings of this sacred circle, we become full of greed, working only for ourselves without truly being sensitive to the needs of anyone else. They recognize that the circle, the birds nest, the sky, the earth, and even the seasons that circle back to where it all begins are all connected.

If we draw a parallel to Jesus washing his disciples feet, it is interesting how the view of leadership and the role that the Chief plays in Native American culture. Even the Christian idea of "He who is greatest among us shall be your servant," can easily be applied. The ways of the Indian Chief meant that he was the "poorest" man in the tribe. When he returned from a hunt, he would give to the widows and the old people who could not go out. Wherever there was a need, he gave away willingly while leaving very little for himself or his own family. That is how the leaders used to live – for the people. Take half a second to contrast that with our American culture of today with politics, CEO and general greed.

Indians look for signs and symbolism. These symbols can come from anywhere: a blade of grass, the feather of an eagle, or within a vision quest. A medicine man that descended from the Bear Clan was sent on a vision quest by one of his elders. Up in the Butte of South Dakota, on the fourth day of his fast, the medicine man returned to share this vision with his elder. "Not a vision or a hallucination he shared, a bear approached me, stood up on his hind legs as he did, I stood up, he tapped me on my right shoulder – a bear is strong he knocked me down, I got up and he tapped me on my left shoulder knocking me once again. I got up and told him that I respected him as a member of my family and that I am not afraid of him. I told the bear he could do whatever he wanted, if he wanted to put his mark on me he could do whatever satisfied him. The bear seemed to listen all the time, then he turned around and walked away."

The elder interpreted this as thus: by standing up to the bear and explaining his courageous spirit, his heart was shown. I relate this story to that of solving our issues even between nations before a war may be necessary. I relate this story to Gandhi's method of non-violence in creating real change. I relate this story to the message and the way Jesus lived his life. Looking for these messages, we not only learn life's lessons, we see the potential for a beautiful world. Though this story is shared under the heading of Symbolism, it could easily go under that of Harmony as well, because it is through our understanding that conflicts can be resolved.

The makeup of a vision quest is interesting and worth uncovering. When sent on a vision quest, and you can apply this to your own life, there are three questions that you must take with you. Seeking the answers in order, the first question is, "Who am I?" In order to succeed in anything you must be able to rely on your own strong identity. The second question is, "What have I become with who I am?" Someone said a long time ago that when life was given to man it was gift from the Creator and what we make of the life is our gift back to the Creator. That leads to the third question of "Why am I here?" This helps lead you to your life's purpose. Seeking the answer to these three questions, you can see how powerful the answers are not only during a Vision Question but carrying them along with us in our everyday life.

Religion

As a Christian, it is interesting to me to hear how the Indian culture today has embraced Jesus. I honestly thought differently until I began to learn and understand. In Indian culture of the past, they recognized every day as a holy day, as a sacred day. Part of their prayer was to let every step be as a prayer, respecting the blades of grass and appreciating it as a carpet that has been laid down for us. They prayed for the children and children of future generations. They considered all forms of life their relatives: the plants, the trees, the birds and the animals.

Stories shared of war can help bring religion into focus. While I think this could relate to any war, the question was asked in World War II (could have been asked from either "side") whether the "enemy" was praying to God? You would think that if you were hearing bullets fly by you that you would find religion real fast. So if we are praying to God and "they" are praying to God, then the question of whose side would God be on would not be relative because you have to believe The Great Spirit or God would be on the side of life. And if we are all worshipping the same Creator, regardless of the actual name we use, might that not put us on the same side? Again, through understanding of worship, I have to believe there is a road to peace.

It was explained to me by Middle Eastern Indians, who use the Gita as their book of religious study and call God by the name of Krishna, that the sun by any other name is still the sun. Regardless of the culture, there is but one God that is worshipped. Native Americans have used terms such as Creator, He Who Gives Life, The Master of Breath, or Ofinga – meaning The One Who Oversees All Things. Whatever name we use, whatever our belief in this area, a closeness to God connects us with something greater, something good, and to all possibilities.

Medicine men may use herbs, chants, songs, prayers, and a pipe, but when you begin to understand their beliefs, all of what they do is to ask power of the Creator. They recognize that the power of the creator is all around us. We all recognize the sun has the power to burn paper, but it doesn't. Only when we focus the power with a magnifying glass does it intensify the sunlight enough to burn the paper. Similarly, the medicine man attempts to focus the power of the Creator.

Harmony

All living creatures and all plants derive their life from the sun. If the sun alone were to act upon animals and plants, then the heat would be so great that they would die. Luckily, there are clouds that bring rain, and the sun and earth work together to provide the requirements for life.

Recognizing the balance of life is required to begin living in harmony. The Indian way is to look at the sacredness of the water and the air while understanding that these elements are required to flourish and needed for the well-being of each generation. The Great Spirit laid out the land like a big blanket, and then he put the Indians on it. As long as the sun shines and the water flows, the land will last forever and give life to men and the animals. There is a fundamental difference between Native Americas and those that came from a European society. Native American Indians could not understand how land could be sold if it does not belong to anyone. The land was like the air and the water. It is sacred; it is given to provide life.

Using symbolism we can look at ourselves as vessels, and everything beginning with us. For ourselves to be replenished and receive more, we need to keep emptying ourselves by giving of ourselves. In this way, we become vessels, holding up one hand to receive the blessings and then opening the other hand to let those blessings flow into the lives of those around us. Your talents and your gifts are enjoyed even more when you know they are being enjoyed by others.

We have seen it presented in movies, and we have read the term in our history books. The Indians were "savages" and living like animals. But the facts are that Indian historians would say they did not see themselves as above or below the animals. They viewed themselves as a part of nature, part of the sacred circle, or as we have coined it: the circle of life.

When we think of war, Indians look to nature for lessons on how to resolve their differences. Take for instance the bear as it wanders great distances for berries and honey. When it comes into a new territory, it seeks the prominent tree where the local bear has made its mark.

When the bear stands on its hind legs, it knows it will have a problem if the mark is a little higher than it can make. We can look to the lessons of nature to seek methods of living in harmony.

It is interesting on how they may respect a ritual, an animal, and even a piece of land to the point of holding it scared. In contrast, America today simply feels that a monetary exchange of some sort should make it alright. Money means power, and everything has its price. Mining companies working through the government have looked to take over the Black Hills of South Dakota, but the Lakota tribe holds this area as sacred. They view this sacred land in the way the Vatican might be viewed as sacred. There continues to be legal struggles over this land, and the government has tried to reimburse the Lakota people, but the elders simply want the land returned. Can you imagine accepting a billion dollars so the Vatican could be bulldozed and the land made available to a mining company? Holding onto a heritage, what connects you to many generations before, or a piece of what makes your community yours, is worth more than any amount of money. This is how we as people plant roots, become grounded, connected, and that is worth more than any amount won in any lottery.

The Indian people viewed the rivers and streams as the veins of the universe, a lifeline that they must care. In contrast, we are afraid to drink from our rivers today. We have not been good stewards of that which was given to us in the purest form.

225

Legalities

Without a police force, judicial system, and incarceration systems, how did these Native Americans keep the peace? The Indian people had a recognized strength of character, and the fact is, like we see in the tolerance of social smoking today, society plays a much greater role in acceptability. Law enforcement within the tribe, called the Light Horsemen, brought the people in who needed to be tried and possibly punished. Within the laws was a strict intolerance for incest, rape, and murder, which all brought a death sentence. If someone stole anything, he received ten lashes. A second offence warranted 20. After the third strike, a habitual thief was faced with the death penalty.

Laws were passed down from generation to generation. They were told by their Fathers to treat all men as they treated us, that we should never be the first to break a bargain, that it was a disgrace to tell a lie, that we should speak only the truth, and that it was a shame for one man to take from another his wife or property.

When someone was sentenced to death, he was given a date, something such as "When this tree casts it shadow on that rock two moons from now, you must be here." The accused was allowed to go home and take care of their affairs and name their best friend as the executioner. Those that warranted such a penalty knew, and they wanted dignity for their family. They did not want to be known as a "coward." That is how they kept up the laws and their enforcement, and as a result the Indian culture did not have very much crime. This continued until the end of the 19th century, when the Indian nation could not execute by way of their own tribal council, and they were forced to accept the laws of the white man governance.

Money

There are many things that represent a stark contrast between our society of capitalism and greed and the peace and harmony of the original American culture. Politics, money, and power, when compared to the culture of the Native American nation, almost seem like one of the greatest oxy-morons in history. The following speech given by Chief Red Cloud of the Oglala Sioux Nation illustrates the contrast well:

> *"Look at me, I am poor and naked, but I am the chief of the nation. We do not want riches, but we do want to train our children right. Riches would do us no good. We could not take them with us to the other world. We do not want riches; we want peace and love."*

It is interesting how Indian culture used wampum, or what we have come to understand as Indian money. It was made out of feathers or shells, and it was made so that it had value. But this value was not necessary of value in exchange for a new shirt or a pair of shoes.

Wampum was used and woven into necklaces and belts and given to honor men such as the chiefs or during a marriage ceremony. Yes, it could be used in exchange for something of value, but one man did not make or gather a bunch of wampum so that he could buy a tipi.

It was not mass produced until the Europeans arrived and discovered that wampum held value to the Indians. The new settlers set a value, that the dark one's were worth more than the white beads, and soon white shells were being dyed. Most of the exchange was made for pelts, but the wampum market lost its value, and the Indians became reluctant to trade. This very well could've marked the first stock market crash in history.

Appreciation

Whenever Indians were to take of the land, whether it an herb, stone, or the earth itself, they gave some sort of offering. Recognizing that everything we use in life comes from Mother Earth, we give thanks. It's not just for the gift of Mother Earth, but to the Great Power that makes all things possible. This respect and appreciation becomes a part of life.

We can provide a stark contrast to this appreciation reflecting back on the earthquake that collapsed San Francisco's Nimitz freeway. You begin to wonder if the engineer gave an offering to Mother Earth, a token of respect that he sees the privilege of building something good on the face of our Mother Earth. Appreciation in all that is given is at the core of our being, appreciation for what others give us, appreciation for what the earth provides completes a circle and a connection to all things.

Look at a blade of grass, which we might walk on every day to pick up the morning paper. As we reach down we may never give that blade of grass a second thought. After all, it's just a step in your day. A fresh cup of coffee awaits, and the delivered newspaper helps start your day. In a way that blade of grass provides a comfort and a beauty to our lives. It also protects us - filtering the air so that we can breathe a little easier. The grass and all its relatives are absolutely crucial to our living. So the next time you step and look down, give thanks to that blade of grass. It was created for your joy. Not only is it there for you to enjoy as beauty in your world, but it is also part of the circle that allows us to live. That little blade of grass has life as much as we do.

Perception

Western movies, and even some history lessons, show Indians as savages. However, the American Indians were exploited, uprooted, and subjected to genocide.

General Custer's last stand and other history lessons give a distorted view of his encounters with the Indian nation. A mere 150 years ago, the Cheyenne people were being forced from their lands and the treaties had been broken. Even the U.S. Indian Commissioner admitted that, "We have substantially taken possession of the country and deprived the Indians of their accustomed means of support." Moving them over 200 miles from the buffalo herd, the Cheyenne people, as means of survival, took aim at nearby livestock which sparked unrest.

Black Kettle was the Chief of the Cheyenne people who sought peace. He made many concessions and an agreement of peace with the tribe's sacred pipe. Chief Black Kettle had a camp set up with women and children when Custer's Scout's had found them. Custer's army waited until the crack of dawn as a woman gathering wood for the morning fire spotted them and reported back to the Chief, who readied the tribe for retreat. Custer's army surrounded them, and even while the Chief had made gestures of peace, he and his wife were shot. Only a handful of children lived through the massacre. Custer returned with the papers labeling him a hero for wiping out a whole band of marauding savages.

Later in the Battle of the Little Big Horn, what came to be known as Custer's Last Stand, the Indian people banded together to fight after continued intrusions into sacred lands. This had been a boiling point. Their women had been raped and their children murdered. The battle cry of the Indian people was, "This is a good day to die." It was a no holds barred type of fight. Today, the Indian people reflect back upon this battle cry and can say, "This is a good day to live".

Some facts that many may not know is that more than 12,000 volunteers were Native American in World War I, which may or may not seem significant if you compare that to estimated population of Indians of 250,000. It may even seem small compared to the estimated 35,000,000 casualties of that war. But Native Americans have done their share in fighting for our current United States Constitution, in addition to all of the sacrifices made of sovereign nations.

Today, Native Americans make up almost 1.5% of the United States population. The Library of Congress uses 900,000 as its estimate of Native Americans before Columbus. As the direct result of written and broken treaties, warfare, new infectious diseases that they had not been exposed to, and forced assimilation, the Indian population was recorded at 250,000 in 1890, and virtually destroyed by the European immigration.

Through our appreciation for one another and the gifts that the Earth provides, and some of the ideas and stories of I am simply trying to point out societal alternatives. Within the circle that connects us we should also recognize each other's unique gifts. By sharing our unique gifts we all enjoy the pot luck of life where we all live in abundance.

Please allow me to share one more story to help illuminate the uniqueness of our gifts. A man had his tire fixed at the local shop, but apparently they did not tighten the lugs properly. Not far from the shop his tire fell off right in front of a mental institution. The car fell onto the axle and it was not easy getting the jack under the car to get the tire back on, but he finally managed. All the lugs were missing, and he was left scratching his head trying to figure out how to secure the tire.

A patient from the hospital had been watching from behind the fence and shouted, "Hey, mister – you want me to tell you how to keep that tire on until get it back to the station?" As you can imagine this man, who had been struggling with this problem was not really in the mood to even really wanting to even humor the patient given the situation But he responded with a rather irritated, "You?"

"Yes, me," he heard

"Alright, yeah. Tell me."

"Take one lug from each of the other wheels, put them on that tire, and it will stay on until you get to where you are going. I may be crazy, but I'm not stupid."

If we value and appreciate the contribution each person makes, then we set ourselves up for a very accepting society where we can feel valued for our talents and hard work. Learn to rise up and to walk the higher path. Abraham Lincoln suffered many defeats in politics. He was even laughed at because he was "ugly." Someone once told him that he looked like an ape, but when appointed President, he appointed that person to his cabinet because he was the most qualified, much like Abraham Lincoln, I believe you have the power within you to build bridges where others cannot see them.

Chapter 8   Plan Execution

Let us take back our government from corporate control and release ourselves from the bondage of a failing economic system.

Does real change come about because a book is written and another person reads it, a song is sung or a speech is given and someone hears it? I believe we have heard enough in the way of empty promises and have experienced enough dashed hopes to realize that the real change we seek will never be realized by electing a new Mayor, Congressman or even a President, regardless of party affiliation. I think we understand that the real change we hope for will only come about when we are united.

But the truth is that it is difficult for us to wrap our heads around the real possibility of change to our culture and society. Even more difficult is that we might all agree on what that change might look like. But the first step is agreeing that the change we seek is systemic and is larger than any one piece of legislation, one candidate or even the best laid out 2400 page federal budget.

We saw the uniting process with Dr. King's movement to equality and for those who remember September 12, 2001, here in United States we as citizens came together with resolve. But it does not take tragedy to unite us; we can unite with purpose, a clear vision and with a desire and hope for real change. With the detailed plan laid out in this book and together we can fix the toughest problems we face as a country and society. The issues of economic equality, corporate power, government distrust and even our own country's impending insolvency or severe austerity that is destined to disrupt the world balance as we know it. The book and this detailed plan of execution gives us a page to work from, this gives us an opportunity to unite with resolve.

There is really only one way to truly make systemic changes to our government and if we are to make any changes to our economic system and it can only be accomplished by amending the document that binds us. Before we review specifics of the constitutional amendments we are proposing and the process of how we the people influence this change, let's be crystal clear about the goals we hope to accomplish and what we are agreeing on:

1. To build a bridge of trust back to our own government
2. To correct all of the problems associated with our current economic system.

If we can agree that these are worthy goals worth pursuing, I believe we can agree that the changes we seek must affect our government system so that we once again have trust in our own representative method. While we are looking at the design of our government, let's frame a government where we can capture the creativity and the voice within "we the people", the citizens of our country. I believe we can also agree that if we are to be successful with government change that the changes we seek must also have a profound effect where our economic system is not limiting our systems of governance the services we wish to provide ourselves as citizens of a community. Profoundly we appreciate each of our contributions, the way we treat and interact with one another. This change should strike at the root of helping build stronger families, connecting us to community and helping each of us to foster our own self-actualization so that we can make our greatest contribution as our true self. This is the promise of the plan laid out in this book. This chapter is dedicated to the execution of this plan.

If we can agree that this is a worthy place to begin, then we can take a collective breath and open ourselves up to real possibilities, real societal change here in the United States. The beautiful thing about the country we live in is that at the roof we are a free nation and within our Constitution, that document that binds us as a people we find a method where we as the people can influence the change we seek. It is also worth noting that it was intended by the authors that it be modified to best suit the times. We can give thanks to the founders of this government and give respect the true native spirit of this land.

Gandhi said that you must be change you want to see. While I can see the point and I do hold Gandhi in the highest regard, I would argue that one person spending more wisely does not make a country less spendthrift or because I exercise it does not help everyone become healthier and/or curb medical costs. Systemic change is something we as a people control, it is something different, and it can be accomplished when we are together in resolve. Because the truth is we want everyone to go to Disneyland, we do not want a system that isolates as if on an island. What we would like to see is us being a part of the best country grading on love, reverence for life and an appreciation for the unique gifts we give each other.

If we can agree that it is time for real change in the United States and understand that it will require us to actually be united to make the change we seek, then what we do when we are united and how we get there are the questions we wish to tackle within this chapter, with this book and with actions put into motion. But before we review specifics let's address the fear that some may have that the reality of the change we speak of here is simply impossible. We are not trying to eat an entire elephant for dinner in one sitting. Actually the question you should be asking yourself is, is would you like this to be possible? If you do, then your signature puts the wheels in motion – that's it, that is all we can do – that is the one bite each of us can do – if we really want to eat the elephant. To find out if there are enough willing individuals to join in this cause – one person at a time, starting with your decision and your signature on our petition we will grow a movement. Before we move on to specifics, let us review a couple of the specific as to why it is necessary now for real systemic change.

Trust in Government

It seems as Americans citizens we have lost faith in our own democracy, our own system of government. This government that is supposed to be in-place for the people by the people is almost used as a punch line now. Please review the gallop data below to review the trend of trust in our government over the past 20 years. This data quantifies what each of us simply accepts as common knowledge, that corruption is widespread and our government acts in the best of interest of their corporate sponsorship and their own re-election.

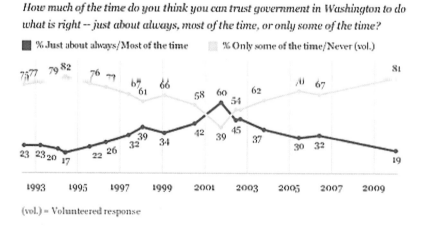

How much of the time do you think you can trust government in Washington to do what is right -- just about always, most of the time, or only some of the time?

■ % Just about always/Most of the time   % Only some of the time/Never (vol.)

(vol.) = Volunteered response

The chasm of trust for our own government continues to widen as shown by this Gallop Pole study data.

Economic Inequality

The below data shows the other major data point of why we seek the change we are asking. The chasm of haves and have nots is detailed in this data presentation of wealth distribution.

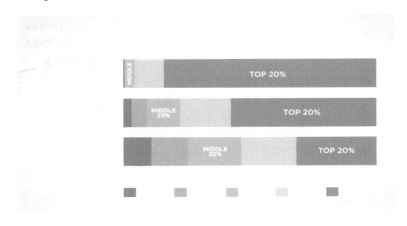

The above graph from a University of Santa Cruz study illustrates wealth distribution, what we as Americans believe would be ideal, what we think it looks like and what it actually looks like. I think we can see the reality is that the chasm of wealthy and a middle class living comfortably is growing and is much larger than we had hoped.

Wealth inequality strikes at the very root of the public unrest with demonstrations such as Occupy Wall Street, of the 1-2% of the well off and the new in general whether it is local or world, we all our left scratching our head thinking there must be a better way. But corporate control and big money influence continues to gain control not only of our government but of our very lives through media manipulation and the ability of us to provide for our families.

After reviewing the reason as to why we should be creating social change, if we are ready, let's take on the how we become united and what do we do to create the change we seek. The instrument we use is our signature placed on your state petition. You may ask why it needs to be a state petition. Well, because that is the method that is granted to us as the people of the United States by our Constitution that allows us as citizens to influence the amendment process. As citizens of our individual state we must petition our State Legislation to call for an Article V convention for the for the purpose of drafting a bill with three amendments that we specify, and that we as the people would vote on in the following general election.

In previous chapters we have discussed the problems of our current economic and government paths, we have provided details of the solution tied to the 3 amendments, provided an explanation of the ideology and the principles based on some of the greatest teacher's mankind have ever known. The truth is that anyone who teaches love, respect and appreciation for his fellow man is represented within the framework of the changes we seek here. Our current level of trust for our own government, the current influence of our economic system has in effect affected our ability to the right to life, happiness and the security that we as a people desire for ourselves.

So, to this point, we understand that the time is now and the current conditions warrant systemic change and it is united that we must stand.

If we can agree that the goals are worthy of our support then with our signature we can find out if there are enough of us like-minded people that we can begin to unite behind a plan to accomplish the change we seek.

By supporting the petition enclosed in this book or online, we must be honest with ourselves in the understanding that we are supporting systemic changes to our society and in it a different way of thinking. You must agree that you can live in a society where we truly appreciate each other and where we as individuals are willing to help out where needed whether it might be coming together to pick tomatoes during the harvest, meeting down by the river to move sandbags during time of flood or just being a part of one of the factories that make up your community. The truth is that we can not only survive but thrive in a society that share's in everyone's unique talents, intelligence, creativity, willingness to help and an open market of abundance in which to do it. We can create change to where not only job stability, economic stability, help wanted and appreciation for one another grow and thrive but we as individuals can look for creative ways to add services that we offer each other, within our communities giving us all the greatest chance being the best we can be, there shall be no victims of the systems.

Our petition to our individual state legislators is to call for an Article V Convention with the sole purpose of drafting a bill to contain the following three amendments:

1. Abolishment of the Electoral College
2. Modification to the Legislative Branch of Government where we the well-connected people of the United States will assume the role of the House of Representatives
3. Acceptance of the contribution economic system

We are given this power of change within Article V of our Constitution. This is the vehicle and it is where we the people working through our individual states can have this profound influence. By signing the petition we show everyone that we are open to the possibility of real change, and our petition gives everyone the opportunity to unite from the same page. Our petition provides us a place to unite and it provides a place of clarity, direction and commitment.

While an amendment has never been created nor has a Convention ever been called by the application of its states, it is the only true lawful means of change. With this path there is a clarity in our resolve and a clear method of non-violent means by which we the people remain in power of a government that reveres it's own Constitution. Please remember the Constitution begins by declaring that this document where we agree, "we the people" we can honor this and give truth to the statement while maintaining the integrity of the document.

Article V of the Constitution reads:

> *The Congress, whenever two thirds of both Houses shall deem it necessary, shall propose Amendments to this Constitution, **or, on the Application of the Legislatures of two thirds of the several States, shall call a Convention for proposing Amendments**, which, in either Case, shall be valid to all Intents and Purposes, as Part of this Constitution, when ratified by the Legislatures of three fourths of the several States or by Conventions in three fourths thereof, as the one or the other Mode of Ratification may be proposed by the Congress.*

Within our petition we provide further clarification as that we are not only petitioning our states to call for this convention to draft the 3 bills detailed, we are also providing clarification that we the citizens shall vote as the provided mode of ratification. If supported by a public vote of ≥ 75% in three fourths of the states than the amendments shall be passed into law, made part of our Constitution and provide the launching point for systemic change that would set us on a path to a new kind of freedom, a new kind of counting and a new kind of world.

There are too many problems that are simply a product of our current economic system. With the change to our monetary system we remove the restrictions of budgets shortfalls and immediately provide a framework for solutions to toughest issues concerning our country;

243

income inequality, healthcare, social security, medicare, our national debt, overcrowding prisons, immigration, homelessness, hunger, poverty, unemployment, a decent retirement plan for all of us and the list goes on. A solution to these problems is the guaranteed promise with the changes we seek.

The truth is our economic system is now working against us. It works against how we are hard wired as humans, against our growing efficiencies, against our desire to live within a stable environment that offers security and our inner desire to serve others. This is why we dread the thought of Universities making millions of dollars as part of the NCAA tournament and argue about the value of the athlete and how we feel it may be exploitative. That is why we want the little guy to do good and then when we see the boy from Brooklyn create a chain of coffee stores we hold him in contempt for pushing the little guy. ON the fact our penal systems I outlined with hypocrisy – if a millionaire gets a speeding ticket for $124 he might want offer the officer cash on the spot, for someone who is trying to figure out to pay rent it might be an entirely different effect. The monetary system sets about a string of contradictions and endless supply of issues that simply do not seem right.

If we allow ourselves, we can focus on serving as much of the marketplace as we can. The truth is your shop or service would no longer compete, like companies will be working together within your community could serve the entire market. The bottom line is all you can do is all you can do. If for example you are a pizza delivery business and you got a 100 calls one night and you had to say no to 19 of them then serving 81% of your market place is good enough As the serving entity you choose who and when to serve, this is what fosters an appreciation for one another. Let us not forget with the pizza delivery scenario that you are working with other services as a whole to provide service to the market.

The Contribution system as a means of economic exchange is not only in line with how we are designed as people but it's in line with the teachings of Dr. King. If we listen inside when we hear his most urgent and persistent question of "what are you doing for others" we either are doing something now or we want to be in a position to serve. The Contribution system puts a system in place that allows us to answer this question for one another. The truth is that which we are giving is typically enough.

With the changes in our government we simply have a real voice, we the people are truly part of the checks and balances and our creative ideas have a platform to gain merit. But Let us be clear, the government change we seek is really what was intended. The House of Representatives was designed to represent the will of the constituents that they represent. At the time of its design it made sense to elect a representative to speak for the people of the region. Now our communication system is such that it allows us to capture our will in real time. For those of us who appreciate leadership within the government, let us also be clear that we don't wish to replace leadership, we need visionaries, we need men and women who inspire, who lead and we need creative ideas that fuel methods of sustainable goods and services.

As the well-connected people of the United State the time has come where we can use the technology not as a means of greater competition to ourselves but to bring a unity and a platform to the give merit to our voice. What I see as the well-connected is the chance to be involved. On a monthly basis, you would go online to vote on matters of community. Your community would include your; neighborhood, school, town, county, state and country. Making your voice an active part of the process we would see of percentage of eligible voters participating and we would at some levels where community leadership goes against the will of the people. We could use this information to either become more educated on why or use this information the next time our elected officials comes up for re-election.

At the federal level where we seem to have the most distrust we the well-connected people become part of the checks and balances. We become part of the reasons why bills are introduced with the aid of the House ambassadors or why a bill is bypassed or denied the right to being a law.

Where I think we can agree is that we would like to build a bridge of trust in our own government, we want the "we the people" to mean something. What we are proposing here is simply a modification to our framework of government where combined with economic change we can focus clearly on solutions and that to which will our individual communities great.

Assuming the responsibility of survival without the threat of money, the burden our survival as a species and leaping over the chasm of fear that comes with a change such as this is something we must all do if this is to be realized. That is something only you can decide for yourself. You must look to yourself as to whether you want an option to participate in a government that takes value in the voice of the individuals within its community. Just try to visualize yourself within this newly structured society, how would you function and would you be willing to help make your community a successful and valued one?

We want a society that allows us to truly be a part of the community through helping our neighbor, helping mankind, and giving the love for our fellow man and woman with a goodness that resides in all of us. But we do need a stick, a carrot and the promise of getting everything you want with the power of "No" also at work. Being part of a community it is time that our technologies and efficiencies make us all better for that which we have created, instead of creating instability and greater competition where we don't know whether our jobs and livelihood will be there tomorrow let us share in our greater resources.

Let's continue down the path of how we get there. How do we get the word out, how do we create a real grass roots movement? We seek the chance to share our plans and ask for support, support of our families, that of organizations, of churches, of companies, of our Cities, Counties and States. We seek to share this idea at every level whatever you're a part of let's share and see if we get others to join in this petition.

Every chance we have at exposure of the message of this new path and let's give everyone a chance to walk on it. We must present this in the most loving and caring way and always with the spirit of non-violence. Let's be clear we are not selling anything, we are asking each other for support of real change by signing a petition with the intention to align a society with who we are as people and to unlock our abilities to give each other a world and a community that is committed to appreciation and sustainability. This movement is such that we seek and appreciate the support of everyone willing to be united in an effort to create a society that is loving and appreciative of each other as we see the connection to our communities.

Let us create rallies, attend festivals, stand outside of grocery doors, and share the message of *A Different Path* with our neighbors. Let us march onto to City Halls and State Capitals where we make petitions available or present copies of completed petitions to ensure that our communities, our state, and our country know that we are united in this path of real change.

There are plenty of ways to become involved, and the truth is we seek your creative contribution and your willingness to help. Ways to help may include organizing events, help with marketing, running sound for a convention, or becoming a presenter. We need to share the petition, at events, through social media, through our emails or attend one of our concerts. I am sure there are plenty of creative ideas that I haven't thought of that you might be thinking reach out your ideas through our website and let's build a network of us that would like the chance to walk down a different path here as it is on Earth.

Whether it is politicians helping form the legislation, or lawyers, doctors, farm workers, factory workers, daycare providers, and students, each of us have a valuable contribution to the whole. The truth is your creative calling may be something we never considered, with each new person becoming involved this movement takes on a new dimension and we could use all the depth and dimensions willing. Let us show the world a path to a new world order, one of love, compassion, creativity and appreciation for one another. We appreciate your willingness to listen, to understand and to get involved. Please use the website and reach out (www.adifferentpath.us) with your ideas and become connected to this movement.

We are setting out to allow the grass of change to grow and to blanket America through this new age in communication advancement, the task of sharing information to the world is available to us all. Our goal is a petition for each state with a 1,000,000 signatures for a convention. We seek this change and your support of the movement. With our signatures we are clear about our intentions and the demand of our state legislators to call this Article V Convention so that we may have the opportunity to vote on a the three constitution amendments we outline here restructures the systems in which we live. It makes us dependent on each other in a good way

We are clear on our intentions for that calling this Constitutional Convention. Let us remove the debt we are giving to our children and forgive those that have given it to us. Let us clean up the dysfunctional bipartisan system of government, let us let go of an economic system that is failing and a government system we no longer trust. We can no longer hope that our children may come up with a solution. We must be the generation, and we are already late to steer the ship that is our society and how we care for one another.

As one person, I can outline a vision, I can share details, I can present the concepts and basis for change as best I can. I will help lead and really help any way I can. All of my efforts in truth, hoping that you find this cause worthwhile, and give careful consideration to using appreciation as our currency to give. It is only if we can think for ourselves and open ourselves up to the thought there may be others. Through your support and us banding together a movement begins on our path to real change grow, through your willingness to help does it grow.

As the movement gains momentum and we near our goal of 1,000,000 signatures per state, we shall schedule a march to the steps of Lincoln Memorial to read newly revised Declaration of Independence presented here. It is simply an updated revision of the original document that united us in our initial struggle for freedom. Updated to suit the times and address the issues of our time as we are no longer worried about the taxation without representation by King George. We the people stake to reclaim our government for the people, by the people, and build a bridge of trust back to our own government in addition we recognize the advancements we have made as a people and the door it has opened in the way of a alternative to our failing economic system.

Declaration of Independence

When in the course of human events it becomes necessary for one people to reshape the political bands which have connected them and to assume among the powers of the earth, the separate and equal station to which the Laws of Nature and of Nature's God entitle them, a decent respect to the opinions of mankind requires that they should declare the causes which impel them to make changes.

We hold these truths to be self-evident, that all men are created equal, that they are endowed by their Creator with certain unalienable rights that among these are Life, Liberty and the pursuit of Happiness. — That to secure these rights, Governments are instituted among Men, deriving their just powers from the consent of the governed.

That whenever any form of Government becomes destructive or even distrusted of these ends, it is the Right of the People to alter or to abolish it, and to institute their rights of born free people.

Government, laying its foundation on such principles and organizing its powers in such form, as to them shall seem most likely to affect their Safety and Happiness. Prudence, indeed, will dictate that Governments long established should not be changed for light and transient causes; and accordingly all experience hath shown that mankind are more disposed to suffer, while evils are sufferable than to right themselves by abolishing the forms to which they are accustomed. But when corruption and self-interests overcome the will of the people pursuing invariably the same object clearly demonstrate a design to reduce them under gained corporate influences, it is their right, it is their duty, to make amendments to such government as intended in its design. — Such has been the patient sufferance of these states; and such is now the necessity which constrains them to alter their systems of Economics and Government. To prove this let facts be submitted to a candid world.

- *The system of competition is misaligned with our innate desires as individuals to give as contributors to our community, our towns, our counties, our states, and our country.*

- *Our financial system, national debt and unfunded obligations have reached critical levels with restraining budgets at all levels of government restricting our own ability to respond to the needs of our community, our towns, our counties, our states, and our country.*

- *Corporate influence has become misaligned with the protection intentions of the Constitution constituents and this influence is contradictory to our government acting on the best intentions of its people.*

Our desires are made in that the government of the people be a servant of the people and to which end this is not provided, then it is in the rights of a free people to speak out and to make amendments to the Constitution to realign the systems to the desires of its citizens.

We, therefore, the people and representatives of the United States of America, assembled, appealing to the Supreme Judge of the world for the rectitude of our intentions, do, in the name, and by Authority of the good People of these United States, solemnly publish and declare, that our rights ought to be a country based on freedoms and liberty for its citizens. That the State Legislators and Federal bodies shall call for a Constitutional Convention in which the following three amendments be made to rebuild trust in our government and to provide a structure in which we all shall enjoy the abundance as intended by our creator aligned with our nature.

1   *Abolishment of the electoral college*
2   *Replacement of the House of Representatives with the well-connected People of the United States*
3   *Acceptance of the Contribution economic system*

And for the support of this Declaration, with a firm reliance on the protection of Divine Providence, we mutually pledge to each other our Lives, our Fortunes, and our sacred Honor, so help us God.

With a clear plan, focus, and direction that truly address the issues of our society today, we can unburden our tomorrows from the ill mistakes while at the same time embrace the advances of yesterday and today. We have in our hands the opportunity to move forward, to flourish, and enjoy the abundance that surrounds us. The abundance we will all enjoy is because of our innate desire to see our work and our efforts appreciated by another and the fact that we are needed will fuel the work being done to sustain.

The framers of our Constitution did the very same thing when they called for a Constitutional Convention only they created an entire societal structure. That accomplishment was not done without duress and controversy. It is clear that they recognized the needs for checks and balances, and within that they also saw a need to provide a means for the people to provide a check of the federal government and make changes if necessary. It has become critically necessary to make systemic change due to the strangle our economic system has along with the level corruption and distrust we have in our government, and within your hands are the instrument and clear vision in which to make this real change reality.

Enclosed in this book, you will find a petition. The secret is in copying the petition and using the power of exponential growth. If you gather signatures, find 10 more people to gather signatures. Soon we will have a 1,000,000, and we will show the world what real change is!

Check out the website (www.adifferentpath.us) for your State's central office location for the address of where to send your signed petition. Please help by signing, by helping get sheets signed, and by making copies of the signature pages and passing them out to those willing to get involved. With the power of exponential growth, we can have our million per state relatively quickly. Let's get started!

What if 2/3 of the states apply for this convention? What if we make a convention happen? What if we create the three amendment bills required to really change our society? And what if we the people vote it into law in the following general election? Then following that ratification, we bring together the technologists that have already created such systems used by credit cards and online exchange to put into place an electronic infrastructure for us to truly become the well-connected people of the United States. Once we have this in-place, then we are ready to make the shift to save our economic system and enact the government structure we can trust and is truly representative of we the people.

When the infrastructure is ready, our balance sheet of debits and credits are frozen following our tax return. The land you own is yours to trade, the boat is yours to keep or share, your bicycle is yours, your credit card statements are yours. These are all a part of your net worth balance sheet that is frozen in hopes that we do not have to return to this financial system that has caused us such discourse.

Following the enactment, competing companies within industries will no longer be competitors they will be collaborators on how to best serve their markets and how best to improve efficiencies and promote sustainability. We will listen to the industry leaders as they share their plan on how they can serve humanity. They will share their challenges, successes, what they will need to serve their chosen field of endeavor, and how their industry will work within the Contribution economic system. No matter the industry, whether it's the apple growers, automobile, real estate, an artist, or the entertainment union, the immediate change will be that those that serve within any given industry will immediately move from competitors to collaborators. This includes those that serve in our local government and those that can work together to provide plans and improvements to our community and outline their minimum requirements for those that they serve.

We shall, in essence, try live the Lord's Prayer. We shall request forgiveness for our debts and those that have debts against us in both the literal financial sense and the emotional sense. And in this way of living, we will enjoy the freedom, the release of bondage, and through it shall come a community filled with love and altruism born of forgiveness, acceptance, collaboration, and giving.

The big question is how do we interact with other countries? How does America essentially separate itself from the world's monetary system? We do it first because we believe as citizens of the United States that there is a better way in that the world would be better served by love and an unbridled sense of altruism. We do it first because America is in the literal sense the leader of the free world closing the gap of haves and have not – this is a worldwide issue and the correcting needs to start somewhere – why not here – why not with us?

So to state the obvious, we as a country, for a while, will need to be self-sufficient. Will that be easy? No. Could it be a little scary? Yes. What we will hope is to be an example for the world to show cooperation, appreciation and pride in community are the answers. As the renewed leader of the free world, we will only be in a position to give of our surplus, not expecting anything in return, just simply appreciating the fact that we are in a position to give or we may find ourselves in a position to barter, say for instance we don't have enough bananas. But the truth is we cannot be afraid of the enormity of this change and how it will affect world economy. We must move forward because it is right and it is time to create a community of love. Trust and cooperation are upon us let us begin by embracing the change that could set us on the path to world peace.

Just like in World War II, for our family members who remember or even the stories we have heard, we must scrimp and save – we must utilize what we have. We will need that person that can help fix our microwaves and DVD players. We telecommute whenever possible. We look to electric cars as alternatives to fossil fuels. We realize that producing and using renewable energy is not just a good idea, but a necessity of sustainable life. No longer are we dependent on any other country. We must be fully self-sufficient, and we must understand that we are and must be a self-sacrificing nation to survive.

We integrate into the rest of the world economy by finding the ways that not only we can serve our communities but the world. Possibly that cargo ship can be given to our Trade Czar, and given that the world will still use the monetary system, we will have to essentially barter our surplus on the open market to help supplement our need for oil or lithium.

What else? What does this system look like? How do we wrap our heads around it? Well, let's come to grip that while the financial sector essentially becomes obsolete, our accounting system of inventories, resources and contributions it becomes like an automated Wal-Mart inventory system. Our efficiencies start to become self-evident, no longer are we serving the dollar in any way, no longer is it necessary for us to mail 100 or 1000 pieces so that we get that one person that may need a new mortgage or credit card. No longer is it necessary to compete and have 50 companies pour hours into a proposal so that the City can select one winner and then have the contract cancel due to budget cuts. Collaboration is so much more efficient over competing.

Our ability to focus on the family sector immediately becomes clear to us because now the focus is now on our family and no greater honor can be bestowed then that of our family being a valued member of the community. Our efficiencies open the door for us to put the focus back on our family unit. We as a society can take stock and value in the role of the homemaker. The value of the focusing efforts in raising our children so that they are well cared for will open the door to a society that I believe we will all come to appreciate.

The door of opportunities opens wide for us, we begin to see the Help Wanted section of the newspaper fill up with meaningful opportunities (if there are people willing to be journalists and help publish the paper). Your dreams become possible and unhindered by economic concerns, no matter if you want to create a candy store, music store, or invent the greatest mop. The only thing that really matters is being appreciated as a valued part of your community. Education opportunities also abound because of the unhindered abundance of resources from willing teachers, books, and abilities to build schools and/or make them available online. We as a society can appreciate someone who is applying themselves with education.

Does this mean everyone can be rock star or play professional baseball? In these cases I believe an organization or venue can help with to provide feedback and/or appreciation. If all you have done is played music with your buddies in the garage for the past year, I personally may be less likely to provide you with my service or you may not meet the minimum contribution requirements for other industries that you may be asking for goods or services of. Using your Contribution Card and sharing feedback to answer the question of what are you doing for others and how are you being appreciated is not so much your currency as it is your ticket to ask for goods and services from others.

The beautiful thing about this system is not only the value that we now place on each other's contributions but the universal we respect we can have for those of us who are aging. Not only are we all entitled to a retirement program, full retirement at 65 and half time after 30 years of service. Accomplishing requirements standards you have earned a sense of entitlement where you have met minimum requirement standards within all industries. Those that are retired can truly offer to give on their terms and organizations can receive an expertise and not be bound by the restrictions of budgets.

How do we align ourselves with the possibility that we can transform a society? How do we cross that chasm of believing that it is possible? The truth is that it is a little overwhelming to think about and our first reaction is that it is not possible. But we have to find out, we have to find out if there are enough like-minded individuals who can say – Yes we would like to change our current course. Simply decide for yourself – sign the petition with the thought of would you be open to being appreciated, guaranteed retirement and an understanding that you will not receive anything unless someone is willing to give it to you. Just like no one will receive the goods or services you provide unless you give it to them.

Changing everything means that we accept the fact that once the last roll of toilet paper is gone, we don't have any. That is, unless there are men and women willing to be lumber jacks in the industry, and that there is someone ready to help transport the materials to a pulp plant, and that there is a community willing to create a factory that will make more toilet paper. Our GDP (gross domestic product) is finite. We will need leaders in charge of industry to monitor, report on production, and help coordinate efforts of efficiencies and resources.

We seek a whole new sense of appreciation for one another, an understanding that no longer will we be working with the system of competition. Instead, we will move toward cooperation, and within this, we unburden ourselves with a competitive/event cut throat industries. The doors open to give valued assistance because you are needed, appreciated and your heart becomes unbridled to follow your dreams and we can live the lives we are meant to live. I see a society close to heaven on earth, a utopia you may call it, but I would say we are trying to promote a way of living that is closer to the Lord's Prayer.

The formula of cooperation over competition will make life more enjoyable, more sustainable, and much simpler. Our societal structure will become more aligned with our innate desire for cooperation and serving our fellow man.

This chapter of plan execution is a working chapter. In this chapter we begin by using the petition in gathering signatures to grow support of state sponsored petitions. As people get involved, as the movement evolves, events, grants, public airings, successes, setbacks and a continued growth of structured plans will continually be updated at the website and social media. Get informed and sign up today to become a part of the movement, to get involved and become part of a real social change. [www.adifferentpath.us]. Everything becomes possible with your signature and if you can open yourself to real change.